M000085883

Evangelical Christians are in urgent need of serious, faithful, and intelligent answers to questions every believer confronts. In this series, Owen Strachan and Gavin Peacock honor the gospel and help believers to understand these urgent questions, to think biblically, and to live faithfully.

Albert Mohler
President, The Southern Baptist Theological Seminary,
Louisville, Kentucky

In this series of books Owen Strachan and Gavin Peacock show us how amazingly relevant the Bible is to our smartphone generation. Technology often only conspires with our wandering and warped passions to leave us in a state of enslavement and despair. However, this trilogy points to God's word as our only hope through its holistic teaching on sexuality and through the gospel of God's redeeming grace. I cannot too highly recommend a prayerful study of these books. They might prove a life-saver!

Conrad Mbewe
Pastor of Kabwata Baptist Church, Lusaka, Zambia

We daily awake to a culture saturated with sexual temptation and confused about sexual identity. Instantaneous and worldwide media accelerate and proliferate these sinful ideologies in an unprecedented way. The Bible, however, provides supernatural power to overcome sexual temptation and divine definition for sexual identity. In this straightforward and powerful series, Strachan and Peacock relay a message of hope, transformation, and biblical recalibration because of Christ. These pages are a reveille bugle to wake up a generation sedated by sinful, sexual trajectories. This series is for pastors, parents, and anyone who desires biblical clarity in a world of confusion.

Rick Holland
Pastor, Mission Road Bible Church, Prairie Village, Kansas

Here is an extremely timely trilogy for the cultural crisis in which we find ourselves. Addressing the issue of human sexuality head on, Owen Strachan and Gavin Peacock have delivered a brilliant analysis of the present day crisis over personal sexuality and gender issues. Not only do they make the right diagnosis, they also prescribe the one and only cure for this devastating problem. They offer the transforming power of the saving and sanctifying grace of God. You need to be conversant with the truths in this trilogy.

Steven J. Lawson
President, OnePassion Ministries
Professor, The Master's Seminary, Sun Valley, California
Teaching Fellow, Ligonier Ministries

I enthusiastically endorse this biblical sexuality trilogy on lust, homosexuality and transgenderism, written by men of conviction, who know what God has revealed in His Word and who understand the sinful struggles of fallen humanity. The authors have courageously written about some of the most sensitive issues of our times, denouncing the deviation from God's original design, while always pointing to the person (Christ) who can give us the victory over such sinful desires and behaviors. If there was ever a generation in need of such a trilogy it is ours. What an insightful and powerful tool this will prove to be for the church of our time. These books are biblical, readable, practical and answer many of the questions many are asking. Every pastor, every leader, in fact, every person who wants to be thoroughly informed about these issues should read this trilogy.

Miguel Núñez
President, Ministerios Integridad y Sabiduría
(Dominican Republic)

Strachan and Peacock confront sexual sin where it begins: in the heart. These men understand that Scripture, by the power of God's Spirit, is the only instrument that can confront the sinful lusts that reside in the dark crevices of the heart. With biblical precision and pastoral care, Strachan and Peacock demonstrate the connection between heart desires and sinful behavior. You would do well to heed their biblical warning and instruction to tackle sinful actions by practically confronting sinful desires with the truth of God.

T. Dale Johnson, Jr.
Executive Director, ACBC
Associate Professor of Biblical Counseling,
Midwestern Baptist Theological Seminary, Kansas City,
Missouri

Our twenty-first century world is deeply confused about the meaning of sex. ... This series directly applies biblical truth to urgent matters of human sexuality, and does so with both pastoral sensitivity and theological integrity. All too often the church fails to respond to sexual sin with both compassion and clarity. This series does both, and does so with courage, verve, and an ever-present reminder that Jesus Christ is making all things new.

David Talcott
Assistant Professor, The King's College, New York

This biblically-centered and theologically-robust series on biblical sexuality is a tour de force. There aren't two other theologians I would rather hear from on these vital issues than Strachan and Peacock. Not only do they bring scholarship to bear on the predominant conversation of our culture, but they offer warm pastoral counsel as they seek to redirect this conversation from the public square back to the foundation of Scripture. If you struggle with sexual sin, deal with questions about sexuality in your current ministry context, or desire to learn more about such issues, this trilogy of books is for you.

Dustin W. Benge
Senior fellow, The Andrew Fuller Center for Baptist Studies and professor at Munster Bible College, Cork, Ireland

Today people are wandering in a fog of confusion regarding sexuality. Truth cuts through the fog in this series of books from Owen Strachan and Gavin Peacock. They have laid out the simple order of biblical teaching on the most contested debates about sexuality. Testimonies and frequently-asked-questions illustrate the practical usefulness of the bible's teaching. I have witnessed the compassion, wisdom and usefulness of this teaching being applied in Gavin's ministry at our church. The result is that these books are floodlights in the worldly storm. They don't claim to be exhaustive, but neither are they exhausting. They offer much-needed confidence to regular Christians on pilgrimage in this new dark age. But most of all, this trilogy highlights the compassion of Jesus Christ in the gospel. Read these books, share them with others, and let hope pierce the present darkness.

Clint Humfrey
Senior Pastor, Calvary Grace Church, Calgary, Alberta

This is a timely trilogy, and a manly one that ladies will also love. Name three topics hotter than these today in society, and any areas where the Christian home and Church more urgently needs equipping than in matters of gender and sexuality? I've already begun walking through this series with my sons, and it has sparked great discussions. Pastor Peacock and Scholar Strachan form a rare combination and a dynamic duo in this thoroughly biblical response to the 'strong winds of culture' that are blowing. They offer not just a 'battle cry', but also a 'declaration of hope'. With a high view of Scripture and of the local church, and a right view of humanity, they bring gospel remedies and clear answers to the most thorny questions. The FAQs alone are worth the price of each book!

Tim Cantrell
Senior Pastor, Antioch Bible Church & President of Shepherds' Seminary in Johannesburg, South Africa

In a world where sex has become everything, anything, and nothing, Strachan and Peacock do a masterful job at helping the church recover and keep a Biblical theology of sexuality. Their series reminds us that God is the author of life and He has not released His copyright on the creation. Sex is His gift, gender

His distinction, marriage His idea, and true love His nature. Any definition of sexual identity or pursuit of sexual intimacy cannot be rightly achieved apart from obedience to God. As the authors argue, the path to true sexual fulfillment is one decided by the gospel, not our glands. In a sex-crazed world, here are wise words that are timely, truthful, and transformative!

Philip De Courcy
Pastor of Kindred Community Church in Anaheim Hills, California;
Bible teacher on the daily radio program 'Know the Truth'

The terrible times of the last days are dominated by 'feel good' culture which has misled millions onto the destructive super-highway of illicit sex in its different forms. From Scripture, research and the experiences of individuals Peacock and Strachan expose the lies that tried and tested societal norms are bad and 'follow your heart' is good. This series is humble and hard-hitting – saying what needs to be said but which many Christian leaders have been afraid to say. However, this is no mere condemnatory diatribe pointing the finger. These pages are full of compassion. There is practical help for those struggling and a triumphant note that though sexual sin is overwhelming the power of the Lord Jesus Christ is greater. This is a very valuable piece of work.

John Benton
Director for Pastoral Support at the Pastors' Academy, London Seminary, London

Owen Strachan and Gavin Peacock are men full of biblical wisdom and conviction. And that's precisely what the church needs in this hour. The authors bring their wisdom and conviction to bear in this work as they engage some of the most pressing issues confronting the church. I heartily recommend this work to every gospel minister—and the church members they serve.

Jason K. Allen
President, Midwestern Baptist Theological Seminary & Spurgeon College, Kansas City, Missouri

The gospel of Jesus is good news not only because it secures eternal life for the believer, but also because it transforms this life, here and now. This is no less true with respect to the contested intersection of gender, sex, and identity. In this trilogy, Strachan and Peacock show how the gospel renews fallen sexuality and brings wholeness according to God's good design. Anyone curious about what the Bible teaches on sexuality and what biblical obedience looks like will want to use these pithy volumes to grow and disciple others into faithful maturity.

Colin J. Smothers
Executive Director, Council on Biblical Manhood and Womanhood

WHAT DOES THE BIBLE
TEACH ABOUT
LUST?

OWEN STRACHAN & GAVIN PEACOCK

CHRISTIAN
FOCUS

Copyright © Owen Strachan and Gavin Peacock 2020

hardback ISBN 978-1-5271-0476-1
epub ISBN 978-1-5271-0581-2
mobi ISBN 978-1-5271-0582-9

10 9 8 7 6 5 4 3 2 1

First published in 2020
by
Christian Focus Publications Ltd,
Geanies House, Fearn, Ross-shire,
IV20 1TW, Great Britain

www.christianfocus.com

Cover by Peter Matthess

Printed and bound
by Gutenberg Press Ltd, Malta

CONTENTS

Dedication

To Al Mather and Alistair Bolt

*Pastors who stood as
watchmen on the wall*

All Scripture is breathed out by God and profitable for teaching, for reproof, for correction, and for training in righteousness, that the man of God may be complete, equipped for every good work.

(2 Tɪᴍ. 3:16-17)

INTRODUCTION

Lust is a problem. A big problem. If you've picked up this little book, you probably know this already. You may have a variety of reasons for engaging with this text. Perhaps you're not a Christian, but you're intrigued by what the Bible teaches about this important subject. Perhaps you're struggling with lust and you recognize—rightly—that you need something stronger than self-help or positive thinking. Or maybe you're a believer but you see that you need to conquer this battle. People are in all sorts of situations today, but here is a constant: many of us need help.

Don't take our word for it. Consider some of the following data on pornography usage, for example. According to a 2018 report in *Psychology Today*, a group of respected psychologists found that 73 per cent of women and 98 per cent of men reported internet pornography use in the last six months. This means that 85 per cent of respondents had used it. The numbers on pornography use in the last week were lower but still startling: 80 percent of men and 26 per cent of women.[1] But lest we think that men alone struggle in a big way with illicit sexual desire, we recall the global book sales of the 50 *Shades* series, sales numbering in the tens of millions driven—as *The Guardian* has asserted—by female purchasers.[2] Clearly, lust is not only a male problem. Far from it. Women have strong sexual desire in them, and they fail to channel it Godward just as men do.

Back to pornography. The website 'Pornhub' is a major outlet for pornography consumption. Here is some noteworthy data listed by the site itself:

- 2018 saw the proportion of female visitors to Pornhub grow to 29 per cent, an increase of three percentage points over 2017.

- The average worldwide Pornhub user is now 35.5 years old. Together, millennials aged eighteen to thirty-four make up 61 per cent of Pornhub's traffic.

---

1 Grant Benner, 'When Is Porn Use a Problem?,' *Psychology Today*, February 19, 2018, accessible at https://www.psychologytoday.com/us/blog/experimentations/201802/when-is-porn-use-problem. Last accessed January 2020.

2 Zoe Williams, 'Why women love Fifty Shades of Grey,' *The Guardian*, July 6, 2012, accessible at https://www.theguardian.com/books/2012/jul/06/why-women-love-fifty-shades-grey. Last accessed January 2020.

- 80 per cent of Pornhub's worldwide visits now come from smartphones and tablets.[3]

Smartphones are changing the way young people are engaging with sexual content. According to Reuters, at least one in four teens are receiving sexually explicit texts and emails, and at least one in seven are sending 'sexts.' These 'sexts' do not always stay in their intended destination. Reuters reported that more than one in ten teens are forwarding these sexts without consent, opening teens up to a storm of embarrassment, exposure, and possibly suicidal thoughts.[4]

The nature of pornography has changed as well. According to the journal *Violence Against Women*, women are being treated aggressively and with increasing hostility in cinematic scenes. In 2010, physical aggression featured in 88.2 per cent of leading pornography scenes and verbal aggression in 48.7 per cent.[5] This aggression was

---

3 https://enough.org/stats_porn_industry. Last accessed January 2020.

4 Lisa Rapaport, 'Teen sexting may be more common than you think,' *Reuters*, February 27, 2018, accessible at https://www.reuters.com/article/us-health-teens-sexting/teen-sexting-may-be-more-common-than-you-think-idUSKCN1GB1XF. Last accessed January 2020.

5 A. J. Bridges, 'Aggression and sexual behavior in best-selling pornography videos: a content analysis update,' *Violence Against Women*, October 16, 2010, pp. 1065-85

aimed squarely in one direction: 94.4 per cent towards women and girls. What a horrifying trend this is. The abuse crisis that has made major headlines across the world in recent years is no stranger to the pornography industry, this is clear. In truth, the two go hand in hand, for pornography trains young men to devalue women and see them as objects.[6]

Other taboos are breaking down as well. In 2018, *Esquire* ran a story entitled 'Incest is the Fastest Growing Trend in Porn.' In the piece, a media researcher named Paul Wright said the following:

> As types of pornography that were less common in the past—for example violence, this or that fetish—become more and more common and easily accessible, consumers get bored by them and need

---

(doi: 10.1177/1077801210382866), accessible at https://www.ncbi.nlm.nih.gov/pubmed/20980228. Last accessed January 2020.

6 Pornography—of the now-common violent and aggressive kind—trains young men in particular to treat women as objects. As Bible-loving Christians, we decry abuse against women of any kind, standing against it in any form, for we have learned from the example of Jesus Christ, the One who gives his body to protect and save His Bride (Eph. 5:22-33). This biblical-theological truth is the single strongest principle against abuse, objectification, and sin toward women that the world has ever known or will ever know. Where abuse occurs for any person (woman or man alike), we encourage both reporting to authorities and involving of church elders so that justice may be done.

the extremity and deviance upped a notch to once again become aroused and excited. Few sexual acts are more extreme or deviant than incest.[7]

Esquire quoted a female doctor who agreed with Wright's point: 'Pornography keeps pushing the boundaries – it's been doing that for a number of decades, to now where it's gotten to incest,' she said. 'Sex has always been about the forbidden, and here it's just about as forbidden as you can get.'

For our purposes, we need to know in Christian terms that the 'forbidden' is anything God disallows, meaning any and all sexual desire outside of the covenant of marriage. But even lost people have a standard of 'forbidden' content. Today, however, that standard is collapsing. Incest is one of the last taboos, generally speaking, in normal human society. Now, it is becoming commonplace in pornography and our sexualized culture.

The Hope of Reality and the Reality of Hope

We could keep going and going, but we'll stop here. We've only scratched the surface of the problem before us today. Lust, of course, drives us toward

---

7   Luke O'Neil, 'Incest Is the Fastest Growing Trend in Porn. Wait, What?,' *Esquire*, February 28, 2018, accessible at https://www.esquire.com/lifestyle/sex/a18194469/incest-porn-trend. Last accessed January 2020.

pornography, but pornography usage is just one manifestation of lustful attention. The foregoing stats show that people are awash in sexual sin. Many have little hope. Our sexualized culture is creating a terrible cocktail of abuse, pain, despair, and suffering. Evil is breeding evil. The traditional barriers that in some way guarded against the full-scale pursuit of lust are falling away. Fewer and fewer people go to any religious assembly[8]; the divorce rate is shockingly high[9]; parents are tuned out from their children; pastors have little to say about difficult matters, and a surprising number disqualify themselves from ministry through sexual sin; society keeps reinventing sex and sexuality; our culture celebrates the destruction of sound principles and traditional norms.

This is not to say that things are unstintingly bad, of course. We do not want to be doomsayers. But we do want to be moral realists. We don't want to pretend everything is great. The fall happened. Satan is real. Sin is a very powerful

---

8 Jack Jenkins, '"Nones" now as big as evangelicals, Catholics in the US,' *Religion News Service*, March 21, 2019, accessible at https://religionnews.com/2019/03/21/nones-now-as-big-as-evangelicals-catholics-in-the-us. Last accessed January 2020.

9 'Marriage and Divorce,' *American Psychological Association*, accessible at https://www.apa.org/topics/divorce. Last accessed January 2020.

force, terrifically destructive, impossible in human strength to contain. Eternal, conscious torment in hell awaits all who do not repent of their sins. People do terrible things to themselves and one another, and shake their fist at God as they do it. This world is not okay. This world is *fallen*.

But the Christian does not dwell in discouragement. We see the promise of salvation and growth in even the most difficult situation. We do so because we possess the Scripture as a gift from God. The Bible is the very mind and will and story of God. The Bible is God-breathed, such that every word is inspired by the Holy Spirit; accordingly, the Bible is inerrant, without error in all it teaches; thus the Bible is authoritative, the standard of all standards; so the Bible is fully sufficient, fitted perfectly to purify us and conform us to God's holy standard. The Bible is not one religious book among many, therefore; the Bible is the very Word of God, the truth we need to form a worldview, understand our lives, and live for God's glory.[10]

---

10 To understand this brief theology of Scripture, see texts like Numbers 23:19; Psalm 119; John 1, 8, and 16; 2 Timothy 3:16; 2 Peter 1:3-11, 21. See also J. I. Packer, *Truth & Power: The Place of Scripture in the Christian Life* (Wheaton, Illinois: Harold Shaw, 1996) and the two helpful statements of the International Council on Biblical Inerrancy: http://www.alliancenet.org/the-chicago-statement-on-biblical-inerrancy and http://

Standing on the Scriptures, we're going to tackle the problem of lust in this book.[11] (See Books 2 and 3 of this trilogy for material on homosexual sin and gender-related sin.) We are a partnership, if you will; Owen is a theologian with pastoral concern, and Gavin is a pastor with theological concern.[12] Our shared goal is not to discourage you. It's actually the opposite. We come with a message of personal transformation grounded in awareness of sin and knowledge of Christ. We're not going to sugarcoat matters; we are going to show you both the bad news of our sin and the good news of the gospel. Knowing both sides of the coin equips you to treasure Jesus all the more.

We will start by covering the darker side of things in Chapter 1. We'll look at our universal problem, sin, in light of divine design as presented

---

www.alliancenet.org/the-chicago-statement-on-biblical-hermeneutics. Last accessed January 2020.

11 In this book, as in this trilogy, we're writing about what the Bible teaches. In doing so, we do not discount other legitimate fields – not at all. But the Bible is our 'norming authority'; in other words, it shapes all our thinking and doing.

12 Owen has invested time and energy in authoring scholarship of various kinds on these theological subjects. Gavin has counseled widely in his church, working with people of various sexual sin patterns (and many others besides), and has seen many people changed by God's grace through the application of sound doctrine.

by Scripture. In Chapter 2, we'll zoom in on the specific problem: sinful desire, the lust of the flesh, seeing that it is a matter of the heart. In Chapter 3, we'll consider how the gospel overcomes our sinful desires, for the gospel is the one force in the cosmos stronger than Satan-powered sin. The power of the gospel is such, in fact, that sin and Satan cannot defeat it. In Chapter 4, we will offer practical wisdom for those who hate lust and want to put it to death. We'll close things with a special section giving some short answers to frequently asked questions (FAQ) based on the content.

Our focus throughout the book is on ordinary, everyday life. We are not trying to produce an exhaustive academic survey; we are not writing a dense theological treatise on internal desire. Such texts are valuable; we even write them from time to time! But this is a book for the church. It's a book for everyday Christians just like us. It's an attempt to help people of all kinds, believers or unbelievers, find their way out of despair and personal compromise. You'll see us reference different sources and voices, and we'll occasionally do a deep dive into key passages or ideas. But in general, keep in mind that this is a book that aims at action. We want to help you know truth, truth that sets you free (John 8:32). This is where hope, true hope, is found: the truth, the truth that is in Christ.

What Is This Book Actually About?

As you engage with the content, remember what we have already noted. The problem of sexual sin is dire, far more advanced than many have acknowledged, but it is not hopeless. We are writing to a wide range of readers, many of whom see that they have a real problem, and that problem is not simply their sinful *actions*, but their sinful *desires*. That's the unique angle of this text (in truth, it's a very, very old angle, as quotations from the Puritans and others will show). If you want to get to the root of the problem, and if you want to overcome helplessness regarding sexual sin, you must tackle sinful *desire*, not merely sinful *action*. Maybe that sounds depressing, but in truth, it's not. It's the very beginning of hope, in reality.

This book is not written for one audience only. We hope you read it if you're a Christian, and that whatever your level of struggle with lust (and there will be a wide spectrum), this is a significant help to you. We hope you read it if you're not a Christian, and that our treatment of this one issue will help you to see much more broadly that you need Jesus in a desperate way. You are not alone here. This is true of us all! Every single human being on the planet has an inexhaustible need for Christ and His sin-destroying mercy and grace. Being honest about your sin, as we will be in Chapters 1 and 2, only shows us how great Jesus is and how powerful His gospel is, as we cover in Chapters 3 and 4.

The situation, to conclude, is very serious. The stakes are not earthly; the stakes are eternal. You can lose your soul by following your lusts; in fact, you *will* lose your soul if you follow your lusts. This is chilling news, but there is something much, much better to consider: Christ is more powerful than any lustful desire, any sin, any temptation. He has defeated death, and He is freeing captives from slavery to unrighteousness (see Heb. 2:14-18).

Turns out in the end this isn't *actually* a book about lust.

It's really a book about Jesus.

1. PEOPLE ARE STRUGGLING

When was the first time you heard the lie?

We've all heard it. We've all been told that pursuing our sexual desires with abandon is freedom. More than this, we've found ourselves whispering this to ourselves, quietly, with no one even around to hear.

If I follow this lustful desire, if I imagine sex with him or her, I'll be truly happy. I'll be free.

But here's the truth: following lust doesn't end up feeling very free at all. When we do it, we end up feeling defeated and lonely and captive. To some degree, we all know this truth personally. Lust is less a fairy godmother granting your every wish, releasing unbounded pleasure and happiness, and more like an iron prison master marching you out to gratify your flesh hour by hour by hour.

This isn't what a sexualized culture tells us, though. Supposedly if we shake off 'repression' of our passions, we'll be fully alive. We'll have ownership of ourselves and our sexual power. We will know who we are.[1] But this exciting language does not prove to be realistic. When our lives are marked by lustful addiction, it turns out that we don't feel like we are in control at all. We do not become masters of our utopian domain. Instead, we end up feeling controlled. Feeling like we are in chains. Though pleasure is what we want, there is actually very little pleasure in the mix. Instead, as we get deeper and deeper into patterns of lust, we feel the opposite of free.

We feel enslaved.

I Can Chase My Lusts (Can't I?)

There are two major ways that lust becomes a pursuit for sinners like us. First, we might struggle with *lusting after the opposite sex* (see book two of this trilogy for material on same-sex lust.) According to many influences all around us— commercials, movies, online images, and much more—when we pursue our passions, you and I will be free. We can chase our lusts with abandon. No one will stop us, and we'll never want to stop.

---

1   We think of what Michel Foucault once said: sex is 'the explanation for everything.' Michel Foucault, *The History of Sexuality*, vol. 1 (New York: Random House, 1976, 1978), pp. 78. While sex is a powerful force, it is definitely not the explanation for everything, and it is not where we will find ultimate meaning.

We will know satisfaction that does not fade, and joy that does not disappear. In addition, when we pursue our lusts, we'll finally attain an elusive feeling of sexual power, sexual control, and reputational impressiveness.

These are powerful urges, aren't they? Voices all around us (including that wild voice in our heart) practically shout to us to go out and get what we want. But as we shall see, this is not how God thinks. This is not what the Bible teaches. And to put it most directly, this isn't actually what happens in our lives.

This is because sin never delivers on its promises. Sin is not God; only God perfectly fulfills His promises. Along these lines, I recall hearing the story of Terry Crews. Crews is a famous actor and an almost-impossibly strong man. He played in the NFL and made millions of dollars in his career. He obtained everything you could want in earthly terms. But there was just one problem with his seemingly perfect life: he was addicted to pornography. 'Every time I watched it, I was walled off,' Crews shared in a video a few years ago. 'It was like another brick that came between me and my wife.'[2] The promise of lust did not pay

---

2   Brandon Griggs, 'Terry Crews: Porn addiction "messed up my life"', *CNN*, February 24, 2016, accessible at https://www.cnn.com/2016/02/24/entertainment/ter-

off at all for Crews, as for so many others. Part of what Crews noticed about himself was how he viewed other people: '[Pornography] changes the way you think about people. People become objects. People become body parts; they become things to be used rather than people to be loved.'

This is a remarkably honest testimony from a famous man. I do not know whether Crews has found true freedom, the faith-driven freedom that comes from repentance in the name of Christ (see Chapter 3). But I do know this: Crews is right about how lust warps us. Children, college students, fathers, pastors, young women, and countless others chase their lusts through visual stimulation. They do this over and over again, often engaging in masturbation, self-gratification, as they do so.

Many people can relate to Crews's predicament – in fact, I think we all can at some level. Of course, we're not all the same. Some are as deep into sexual addiction as Crews was, and are in eternal peril. Others aren't as far in, but still find themselves lacking the self-control they need in this area. You know Christ as Savior, and you want to grow, but

ry-crews-porn-addition-feat/index.html. Last accessed January 2020.

you don't know how to gain mastery over the flesh. Your battle against lust is a series of starts and stops, with some gains, and some losses.

I Am My Sexuality (Right?)

This isn't the only battle men and women fight, though. There is another category of lust that we might be drawn toward. Our struggle can take a second major form when we hunger *to be lusted after by the opposite sex*. You can desire to be desired. We'll delineate an appropriate urge for a spouse in pages to come, but that's not what we're discussing here. In our flesh, we may well hunger and yearn to be seen as sexually desirable—'hot' in common language—by the opposite sex. We try to find our very identity in that coveted label: 'She's so *hot*.' 'She is such a babe.' Or 'he is such a heartbreaker.' The phrases shift with each generation, but the point stands: some of us struggle powerfully with lust in this respect.

To be clear, those who fall into this category may or may not have a major obsession with lusting after others (as outlined above). But make no mistake, lust is *still* a serious problem for many in this way. It's not okay; it's not godly. Our habits, our spending, our time spent getting ready for the day: all this may reveal a major appetite for attention, sexual attention. That might be the end goal—drawing eyes and being pursued—rather than a sexual experience, but it matters not. Sin is fueling this passion.

Not long ago, I read a powerful recounting from a former 'porn star' that made this point. Crissy Moran was from a broken past and always struggled to feel loved. Though a beautiful woman, she never felt like she measured up: 'I never felt good enough for the men I dated,' Moran said. 'I didn't feel beautiful because they looked at porn during sex with me.'[3] This lack of fulfillment, this unstable identity, caused her to hit back at her circumstances, according to her: 'I thought, am I not good enough for you that you can't only look at me? I felt worthless to the point that I chose porn and I said, "One day I'm going to be one of the girls you watch on screen."'

Moran's story shows us that she came to understand her part in this terrible drama. In entering the pornography industry, she entered one of the most dehumanizing modern environments there are. She

---

3   Mel, 'Actress Shares How God Saved Her From Porn Industry,' *Godvine*, accessible at https://www.godvine. com/read/ex-porn-star-crissy-moran-testimony-1701. html. See also Adam Popescu, 'Crissy Moran Tried to Leave Porn Behind, But the Industry Won't Let Her Go,' *The Kernel*, March 27, 2016, accessible at https:// kernelmag.dailydot.com/issue-sections/features-issue- sections/16236/crissy-moran-starting-over-after-porn. Last accessed January 2020.

experienced real evil there, and was shocked by what she encountered. As a Christian reading her story, one cannot fail to see just how deep sin goes, and how abusive it is. Moran's deadening choice brought a harvest of guilt and shame upon her. She later recognized her role in her undoing: 'I blame myself for all my bad choices … And I've made some terrible ones. Terrible. And everybody can see them.'[4]

Moran's experience—one of many such examples of women who have fled the false promises of the pornography industry—reminds us that we cannot find happiness in being sexually desired. This is true whether our family background is shot through with pain or whether we come from a loving home. We are not our sexuality. By this I mean that while our manhood or womanhood is an absolutely crucial part of our being, we were created spiritual beings who were formed for fellowship with God. That is the first truth about us, not our sexual preference. We are spiritual beings, embodied souls, who have been given the joy of living in the world God has made. This

---

4   The story makes this point poignantly when it notes that in entering the pornography industry, Moran signed away many of the rights to her content. To this day, long after breaking completely and publicly from her thriving career, videos and images of Moran are widely available (she filmed more than fifty videos according to Popescu).

first truth—spelled out below—means for us that happiness cannot ultimately come from an identity grounded in sexual desirousness.

We cannot police other people's desires. We are not ultimately responsible for what anyone but us does. But with that important point noted, we can and must watch our hearts. We think of what Peter teaches godly women to do. Instead of loud or provocative dress that draws attention, including sexual attention, the woman of Christ seeks to adorn herself with the fruit of repentance and godly growth (1 Pet. 3:3-4). In doing so, believing women take control of their heart, not allowing it to yearn for the lustful desires of men. If this is true of godly women—as it must be— there is a principle for all Christians to know here.

The preceding discussion leads squarely to a central question: why do we—God-made men and women—misuse such a wonderful gift, the gift of sex? To learn more, let's dip into the witness of Scripture in order to understand why humanity twists the blessing of sex. We'll look at three texts, all from the earliest chapters of the Bible.

You Were Never Supposed to Sexualize Your Identity: Genesis 1:26–28

Who are we as humans? This is really the central question of our time. All sorts of questions are connected to it: are we a creature just like the animals? Are we a blob of cells, evolved from gases? Is there anything fixed and stable about us as people?

Who are we, we ask today? Or more personally: *who am I?*

There's much to say to these good questions. The first truth that we know from Scripture is this: we are unique. God made humanity on the sixth day of creation *in His image*. Here's Genesis 1:26-28 on this count:

> Then God said, 'Let us make man in our image, after our likeness. And let them have dominion over the fish of the sea and over the birds of the heavens and over the livestock and over all the earth and over every creeping thing that creeps on the earth.'
>
> So God created man in his own image, in the image of God he created him; male and female he created them.
>
> And God blessed them. And God said to them, 'Be fruitful and multiply and fill the earth and subdue it, and have dominion over the fish of the sea and over the birds of the heavens and over every living thing that moves on the earth.'

There is a lot here to unpack. We've done some of this work in our book *The Grand Design*.[5] We won't

---

5 Owen Strachan and Gavin Peacock, *The Grand Design: Male and Female He Made Them* (Fearn: Ross-Shire,

retrace all that ground, but we will note this: humanity was designed by God, fashioned by God, and blessed by God. The human race was created specially by the Lord, as Genesis 2 shows. The man and the woman were made to partner in taking dominion over the earth. But that's not all: the original mission given by God was to 'be fruitful and multiply and fill the earth' (v. 28). Here we see that the gift of sex was a key part of God's good plan for humanity. The human race glorified God in a special way by being 'fruitful' and welcoming children into the world.

This shows us that sex is God's invention. No foul mind thought it up. God designed Adam and Eve, the first man and first woman, to fit together physically. He also enabled sexual union to produce children and thus build the family. God clearly intended for sex to be a gift and a means of blessing not only to married couples, but the entire earth. Sex, then, is a good gift of God.

Sexual Desire Is God's Good Marital Gift: Genesis 2:23–25

The good plan of Genesis 1 leads us to the beautiful events of Genesis 2. Genesis 2 shows us the first instance of sexual desire in world history. After the

---

Christian Focus, 2016).

Lord has created the man first (v. 7) and charged him to work and watch over the garden (v. 15), He then creates the woman (vv. 21-22). The woman, to speak frankly, dazzles the man. Though we might read the following silently to ourselves, the text explodes with delight:

> Then the man said,
>
>> 'This at last is bone of my bones
>>> and flesh of my flesh;
>> she shall be called Woman,
>>> because she was taken out of Man.'

Adam exudes a sense of overjoyed relief. This *at last* is the one who fits with me, he shouts. Eve was made from Adam's rib, and so there is an immediate connection here. Eve is not a beast, not a fish, not a monkey. She is one of a kind. She is a woman, an image-bearer like the man, and full of the glory of the Lord. She is his 'helper,' signaling that she will receive and honor and support his leadership even as she brings strengths to the marriage that only she can contribute (Gen. 2:18, 20).[6]

The man and the woman, joined together here in a garden marriage ceremony, are made to desire one another. Verses 24-25 make this plain:

---

6   Note here that the roles of men and women flow out of the design of God and the order of creation (1 Tim. 2:9-15). From our God-given sex, then, flows our God-given role in life.

Therefore a man shall leave his father and his mother and hold fast to his wife, and they shall become one flesh. And the man and his wife were both naked and were not ashamed.

There is no 'shame' in their sexual union, in their nakedness. There is instead delight, happiness, and unfettered joy without any hint of pain, evil, or shadow. The Bible is displaying for us without embarrassment just how beautiful sex is. We learn in Genesis 2 that sexual desire directed at one's spouse is not shameful. It is good and God-glorifying. God intended us to desire a spouse, a person of the opposite sex, if he called us to marriage.

All this matters greatly for us today. We'll talk about the fall in just a moment, but we need to see that the desire to be married is not a bad thing. Wanting a spouse is a good thing in biblical terms, and it is better to marry than 'burn with passion' according to 1 Corinthians 7:9. This means that it is right for a man to want to marry a woman. It is right for a woman to want to marry a man. Not every person is called to marriage. Later in Scripture, we will learn at some length from Paul that singleness is honorable before the Lord (1 Cor. 7). But in God's wiring, many men and women do desire covenantal union (about 90 per cent of people get married in Western cultures).[7] This is because God made marriage, God is glorified greatly in marriage, and God wants our good. We ought never to feel weird or wrong for wanting marriage, whatever our culture tells us.

Many people want to be married, and this is good in God's sight, and to be held in honor by all (see Heb. 13:4). No one should look down on marriage, complain because a church celebrates and champions marriage, or feel inadequate because a local congregation draws many married couples and families. Marriage is the central means of sustaining the human race from one generation to the next; marriage was made by God as the first institution of all society. Marriage, we learn, is a living picture of the gospel (Eph. 5:22-33).

In biblical terms, marriage fills a major role and helps with a major human instinct. Marriage is the outlet for all sexual desire. There is no other arrangement that Genesis or any other biblical book indicate is fine for sexual activity. The Bible doesn't commend sex in a dating situation, a one-night hook-up, a long-term boyfriend-girlfriend relationship, a cohabitation arrangement, a group setting, a virtual fantasy-driven encounter, or

---

7   https://www.apa.org/topics/divorce/ Last accessed January 2020.

any other setup. There is one and only one God-honoring outlet for sexual desire: marriage. God intends for marital desire to drive us into marriage, just as God intends for marital desire to last years, decades, even a lifetime. God is not a squelcher of happiness; he wants married couples to enjoy the gift of sex.

The Lord wants couples to see sex within a biblical framework. Marriage in the biblical mind is a covenant. It's not a partnership. It's not a mutually beneficial economic relationship. It's not a contract. Marriage is a joining together of two people, one man and one woman, for life. Marriage is a sharing of everything – body, soul, goals, joys, trials, and more. It is 'one flesh' union. The design of God is that a man would 'leave his father and his mother' and by God's leading find a wife, a wife he holds fast to and never leaves (Gen. 2:24). The man hears the call of the Lord to leave his dad and mom; he has no such call to leave his God-given wife. He has the responsibility, therefore, to lead, just as he has the responsibility to protect and provide (see Gen. 2:15 again).

All this reveals God's plan for sexual desire. From the beginning, even before the fall, God wanted humanity to express this God-given instinct in the covenant of marriage. He wanted spouses to feel great joy in coming together physically. He created us to find delight in one another's frame, body, personality, care, tenderness, mind, and so on. He did not blush at whole-body, whole-soul union. He made it, and made it for our good and his renown.

But alas, this is not the final word on sex and lust. The biblical story continues, and not happily.

The Fall Brought on Our Shame: Genesis 3:1-7

The reason our vision of sex goes awry is because we followed the words of a snake over our sovereign.

It's true. Genesis 3 gives us the real historical narrative of our collective human breakdown. Our first father and mother trusted Satan over God, and believed his word over the Lord's:

> Now the serpent was more crafty than any other beast of the field that the LORD God had made.
>
> He said to the woman, 'Did God actually say, "You shall not eat of any tree in the garden"?' And the woman said to the serpent, 'We may eat of the fruit of the trees in the garden, but God said, "You shall not eat of the fruit of the tree that is in the midst of the garden, neither shall you touch it, lest you die."' But the serpent said to the woman, 'You will not surely die. For God knows that when you eat

of it your eyes will be opened, and you will be like God, knowing good and evil.' So when the woman saw that the tree was good for food, and that it was a delight to the eyes, and that the tree was to be desired to make one wise, she took of its fruit and ate, and she also gave some to her husband who was with her, and he ate. Then the eyes of both were opened, and they knew that they were naked. And they sewed fig leaves together and made themselves loincloths.

In this passage—a real historical event, not a mythical scene in a play—Satan pitted his word and his promises against God's. He succeeded in getting the woman to believe that God was keeping something good back from Adam and Eve. As she listened to Satan speak—a truly chilling thought—Eve wanted what Satan offered instead of what God offered. So she ate, and led her husband to eat. Adam shamefully failed to step in here and protect his wife from Satan. He failed in his duties, the first man to do so.[8]

---

8 To better understand the play-by-play of the fall, see Owen Strachan, *Reenchanting Humanity: A Theology of Mankind*, pp. 54-83. In sum, Satan is not just getting the man and woman to eat fruit they shouldn't eat; he is setting up a counter-revelation to God, and corrupting all God's good promises and moral teaching. He is instituting a system we can call 'paganism' that emphasizes creature worship over Creator worship.

What followed was knowledge of nakedness (v. 7). Genesis is telling us something important with this comment. In following God's plan, the first couple were naked and without shame. But following Satan's plan meant the first couple were naked and felt great shame. This is always the way it works, then and now. Following Satan's plan brings shame in many forms. Overwhelmed by this newfound sensation, the first couple tried to hide themselves. Distance came between them and between God. Their bodies, created to glorify the Lord and delight their spouse, now seemed flawed and worthy of hiding. Covered in shame, they covered themselves.

We could say so much about how the fall affects human sexuality. We have to limit our comments at present, however, to the issue of lust. Genesis 3:16-19 show us that the marriage relationship is now riddled with sin. God made it for peace, joy, and love. Instead, couples will now struggle with one another. The woman will sinfully try to lead her husband. The man will now sinfully try to dominate his wife. Husbands and wives will not dwell together in harmony and unity. Now, they will battle one another. This was not God's design in any way. But it is the real 'fruit' of eating forbidden fruit.

As a result of the fall, sexual desire will misfire. We will trace this in much great detail in Chapter 2. For now, we can note this: one outworking (of many) of the fall is that the man and the woman will no longer be satisfied with one another. They will now wander in their desires and affections. In their flesh, they will not be satisfied with the spouse God gives them. They will pursue their lusts outside of the covenant of marriage, whether mentally or physically.

The desire for marriage was made by God to be a powerful force. It was fashioned by God, as we saw earlier, to drive a man out of his home and to lead him to take a wife for himself. The man was made for the woman; the woman was made for the man. They were designed by God Himself for physical unity. Their differences of body, temperament, and so on were not bad in themselves, but were given to display unity in diversity. Said more simply, God wanted two who were not the same to become one. He wanted one-flesh union capable of producing children. Only complementary man-and-woman marriage can provide this.

All this order, God-given order, depends first on a man's interest in marriage. Sexual desire is never right outside of the covenant of marriage, but the desire to be married was a key part of the good plan of God for humanity. In reciprocal terms, Eve was made to be delighted in by Adam. She no doubt felt great joy when Adam shouted praise to God in Genesis 2:23 – 'this *at last* is bone of my bone,' he cried. Nothing was wrong or untoward about that shout of delight. God clearly wanted Eve to enjoy her husband's loving attention. This was not a curse to Eve; it was not a neutral reality. There was no hint of wrongness in her welcoming, even wanting, Adam's husbandly desire. Instead, God was richly glorified as things worked as He intended, and the woman's form, feminine demeanor, and gracious receptiveness inspired Adam to praise the Creator.

It pains us to recognize how all this goes wrong in the fall. Now, the man will not rightly celebrate God's kindness in the gift of a wife. Now, he'll grumble at what God has given him. Now, he'll find himself sorely tempted to not love his wife. Now, his eyes will wander, and he'll think hard about whether he should gratify his lusts elsewhere. Similarly, the woman will not naturally welcome the leadership of her husband. She won't take joy in watching him own his God-given role. She'll try to usurp it, chipping away at his authority, undermining him. In her natural state, she'll know that she may well have a certain sexual power over men to some degree, and she'll be tempted to use it against men to get what she wants.

Are Lust and a Desire for Marriage the Same Thing?

We've sketched thus far why things go wrong in sexual terms. But we need to pause for a moment and answer a question that develops from the preceding material. If the fall corrupts us all, does it make all forms of sexual desire wrong? This is a good and natural question, one that theologians have considered for a long, long time.[9]

The fall does affect us comprehensively. Yet there is a difference between God-honoring marital desire and sinful lust. Following Adam's disobedience, we must distinguish between these two instincts. The fall changes our nature but does not change God's design. By this we mean that it is still very much 'natural' to want marriage, and it is thus 'natural' and good for a man to want to marry a wife, and for a wife to want to marry a husband (Rom. 1:18-32 speaks of what is natural and unnatural in some detail; see

---

9   For example, readers should consult Augustine's theology of desire. See the strong work by Jared Moore, 'A Biblical and Historical Appraisal of Same-Sex Attraction,' PhD Dissertation, The Southern Baptist Theological Seminary, 2019. Moore not only addresses same-sex attraction but the issue of lustful desire more broadly; he covers Augustine's thought, with its twists and turns, in no trifling detail.

also 1 Cor. 11:1-16). This is because there is such a thing as 'nature,' *physiv* in the Greek (Rom. 1:26).[10]

In fact, this discussion of what is natural shows us that even if we are not called to marriage, it is still right to keep marriage in honor. There is no glory for God in any 'unnatural' desire, and so even the lifelong single person honors the Lord by embracing their God-given manhood or womanhood. A man should be a man, not given to effeminacy in identity, thinking, or manner; a woman should be a woman, not given to manliness in identity, thinking, or manner. Manhood and womanhood are 'natural' in the biblical mind. (Natural, it seems, is a better term for what we're describing than 'heterosexual' or 'straight' or other alternatives, close as they may or may not be to the mark.) The gospel doesn't make us 'straight' per se, but it does restore us to God's good design for our manhood or womanhood.[11]

---

10 'Nature' is part of what we call 'general revelation.' It tells us something about God's intention for humanity, in other words. There is order in the cosmos, and it depends on nature as made by God. Sin is found in thinking, desiring, and acting contrary to nature and God's will (which are in truth one).

11 For this reason, we must indeed say more than 'The gospel doesn't make you heterosexual, it makes you holy.' There is some truth here, but we must make clear that conversion does indeed enable us to love what is natural

A Framework for Biblical Sexuality

At this point, perhaps it will be helpful to suggest a framework which we can use to discuss God's natural design. There are five parts to our framework for biblical sexuality; some of what we will say below gathers points we have already made.

First, we can identify *complementary unity*. Here we mean what we introduced above: that the man and the woman are made in God's image (Gen. 1:26-28). The man is formed first, and the woman is formed from his body. This order of creation matters, and matters greatly in the life of the church (see 1 Tim. 2:9-15). Even as the order of creation establishes the man's leadership in the home and the church, the sexes alike bear God's image and give Him glory. There are no grounds, then, for any unequal view of men and women; men and women alike possess God-given dignity and worth as those made in the image of God. Men and women are unified in creation, made for a shared mission of dominion in all the earth.

Secondly, we can identify *complementary polarity* in biblical sexuality. Here we mean that the sexes—though fully unified—are made distinct by God. The man and the woman share humanity,

---

and free us from what is unnatural (including effeminacy, lustfulness, homosexuality, androgyny, and much more).

48

but do not share manhood and womanhood. They have different bodies, different bodily working, and different roles and duties that flow from God-given distinctiveness (Gen. 1:27; 2–3). Of course, there is a spectrum of difference between men and women; we overlap in many respects in both creation (God's original design) and new creation (who we become in Christ). Yet we are right to see throughout Scripture (and throughout our own experience in this world) that the sexes are distinct in many ways, and that this distinctiveness is to the glory of God.

Thirdly, whether married or single, every Christian man or woman embraces *complementary reciprocity*. They see that God made the sexes— however distinct— to work together, to face one another, regardless of marital call. Every Christian understands and reveres God's beautiful making of man and woman, and every Christian prizes the gifting each sex bears for different life callings and tasks (Gen. 2; 1 Tim. 5). They honor God's call to Adam and his sons to be leaders, protectors, and providers; they esteem God's call to Eve and her daughters to be nurturers of children, attuned to the home, and supporters of godly men.

Some men and women may not have any desire for or call to marriage, but they nonetheless see themselves as a godly man or woman. They recognize the goodness and blessedness of the opposite sex, and they welcome the distinctive contributions of godly men and women in the shared life of the church (and beyond). Trusting Christ entails all this; it does not mean 'becoming straight' or 'having sexual attraction for the opposite sex' per se. It does, however, mean that we are restored to 'natural' functioning, thinking, and living.

Fourthly, we must also speak of *complementary interest*. By this we mean that as many boys and girls come of age, they will find an interest in the opposite sex developing in them. These stirrings, as we have articulated already, are a key part of how the human race continues to 'multiply' and 'fill the earth' to God's glory. Of course, we are not speaking of any lustful desire here. As we have noted, Scripture does not endorse sinful lust. So we must distinguish here between a 'natural' and innocent interest in the opposite sex on the one hand, and lustful sexual interest on the other.

There is some grayness to this distinction, we admit. Nonetheless, it is right to affirm in our children the development of complementary interest – that is, interest in the opposite sex per the good teaching of God's Word and the natural maturity of the child. We should avoid three errors on this count. *First*, we should not sexualize this interest. While much is developing within the child, we should not equate interest of any kind in the opposite sex with evil passion. *Second*, we should not awaken this interest before its time (Song 8:4). Unlike our non-Christian culture, we want to raise our children with patience and great care, never pushing them into something they cannot handle, shielding and protecting them as we must.[12] *Third*, we should not stigmatize this interest. God is the one who gives boys and girls complementary interest, not any evil being. Even as we should not 'awaken love' early, so we recognize that interest in the opposite sex will emerge as adolescents mature. This is not wrong; this occurs due to the wise design and common grace of God.

We can go further, though. Fifthly, we must also speak of a *complementary desire for marriage*. It is right and holy to desire marriage as an adult. The desire to be married, including the hope of one-flesh union in a righteous way, is good. We should teach this plainly to our children and our churches. At the same time, as noted a minute ago, all sexual desire outside of the covenant of marriage calls for confession and repentance. This is no trifling reality. But with that said, when a man

---

12 We think on this count of how children who have 'trans-gender' desires are encouraged by parents to transition to the opposite sex. This is an extreme example of parental decision-making that is so unwise it is tantamount to abuse.

prays for marriage to one woman, or a woman asks the Lord to bless her with a godly husband, we must be very clear that Genesis 2, Song of Songs, Matthew 19, and Ephesians 5 (among other texts) show us that these prayers of righteous saints honor the Lord and His beautiful design.

We find ourselves in an increasingly anti-marriage culture. We are encouraged by our post-Christian context to delay marriage, have a childless marriage, or do away with the concept of marriage altogether. But in Scripture, marriage is front and center. The Bible effectively begins the story of humanity with marriage in a garden, and it ends with the wedding ceremony of Christ and His Bride in a garden (Gen. 2; Rev. 21). This is deep theological truth, yes, but it is truth that shapes our practical approach to earthly marriage. The desire for marriage is good and right. We do well to train our children to know this and even to have a complementary desire for marriage. We do not want them to languish in loneliness and frustration and sexual temptation when God has made them for marriage.

There is no perfect experience of marriage, it is true. Just as we must not idealize sex in response to a fallen mindset, loading it with more weight than it can bear, so we must not idealize marriage. There is no perfect marriage. Marriage is challenging, and at times it can take us right to the end of ourselves. While confessing this freely, we also must make clear that God calls most people to covenantal union and thus intends for them to find much sanctification and meaning and purpose and happiness in this state. The world says this is not so, but the church holds fast to the good plan of God for the family. From this vantage point, the church needs to work in deeply counter-cultural ways to guide young men and women to marriage – and to help them through the peaks and valleys of the days that follow the happy ceremony.

We need to close our little discussion. From the preceding content, the goal for every Christian of every kind is hopefully clear at this point. The church is not pushing every person into marriage; this violates 1 Corinthians 7 and the God-exalting nature of singleness. Neither, however, are we losing sight of God's complementary design of the sexes, God's development in many boys and girls of interest in marriage, and God's work to nurture a desire for covenantal, complementary marriage.[13]

---

13 Singleness is not the normative state in the church. It is an honorable state and a means—through God-given faith—of glorification of the Lord. But the family established by God forms the basis for leadership qualifica-tion, for example, in the new covenant community (see

Whatever our current state, and whatever our calling, we want to glorify God in thought, desire, and action as the men and women he made us and redeemed us to be.

Conclusion

The fall has terribly and tragically messed things up. Following the fall, we can no longer identify much of our sexual desire as good. We very much hear this argument in our culture today, that our sexuality is inherently virtuous, but it is simply not true. As we just noted, there is God-glorifying desire for marriage that God gives. But there is also sinful lust that the fall introduces as a condition of the depraved human heart.

Following the fall, the man will lust after women who are not his wife. Following the fall, the woman will want to be lusted after by men who are not her husband. In truth, the picture grows more complex still. Both sexes will struggle in different ways with these depraved instincts. No one will be raised in a perfect family, and some will hail from deeply fallen homes, especially as growing numbers of people reject Christ (and as societies move ever further away from biblical wisdom). In

---

1 Tim. 3:1-7). While married and single people alike form the 'household' of God, the family continues to have tremendous importance in the church (1 Tim. 3:15).

any culture, any society, pain will produce pain; sin will produce sin. We are not victims of this process; we are criminals. No matter what pain is in our past, the Scripture teaches us that every person stands guilty before the Lord for their own sin.[14]

It is true that our environments affect us. But much as we are influenced by others, our true problem is not outside us. It is inside us. This confession may sound rather foreboding, rather gloomy, but actually, acknowledging the depth of our problem is the very first step to overcoming it. Now that we know God's good plan and our natural sinful condition, we are freed to laser in on sexual desire. In the next chapter, we do just this: we zoom in on this problem that is common to us all in order to ready ourselves to overcome it. When we know how deeply sin goes, we'll know just how magnificent Christ and His transforming gospel truly are.

---

14 There is no one righteous, no one innocent, for all have sinned and stand guilty before the Lord. This is true without exception, and it is a very strong counter-cultural word. Yet this is the plain confession of Romans 3:10-18, and we dare not edit it, soften it, psychologize it, or lose it.

2. LUST IS SINFUL

When in college, I remember hearing teaching on sexual temptation. When you see an attractive girl, the argument went, you should divert your eyes and move on to other things. I found this practical teaching of some use, but it struck me then and still strikes me now that this step is not enough. Diverting one's eyes is necessary when temptation presents itself. But what, I wondered some years ago, does a believer do about the bigger problem – the fact that we *want* to lust? My eyes, after all, are only doing what my heart desires.

Whether we struggle with lusting after the opposite sex, or with wanting to be lusted after by the opposite sex, we need practical wisdom – all sorts of it. As much as we can get! (see Chapter 4.) But in truth, we need more than that. We need deeper help. We need God to work not only on our daily habits and our momentary behaviors, but to work on our hearts. We want to change our deeds, yes. But even more than that, we want God to change our affections. This is truly the secret to killing lust and overcoming sexual addiction.

Actually, this isn't much of a 'secret' at all. It's not some genius idea. It's Bible 101. In this chapter, we're going to look at this truth in depth. We'll consider first what the Bible teaches about internal sin; second what the Bible says about lusting and being lusted after; third how the Bible links in a smooth chain our thoughts, hearts, and actions. Our goal with this material is not to wallow in misery. Instead, we want to take a close look at the spiritual X-ray of ourselves, and understand how we can most effectively fight lust. Victory is the goal, not despair; transformation, not trauma.

What the Bible Teaches About Internal Sin

Naturally, we want to believe that our hearts are good. But the fall of Genesis 3 stubbornly intrudes on this pleasant fiction. Through the fall, we all gained a sinful nature, one that begins to manifest itself as soon as we're born. No one has to train us to sin; we don't need courses in 'How to Lust 101' and 'Ways to Maximize Efficiency in Wrongdoing.' Our heart, called 'desperately wicked' (NKJV) in Jeremiah 17:9, does wrong without any training. We do not love God by nature; we do not obey God by nature; further, we do not *want* to love or obey God. You can scarcely get more clarity about the pollution of our heart than Titus 3:3, which says that we are naturally 'hated by others and hating one another.'

The typical place to locate sin is in our behavior. We can all recognize that we do certain things that we shouldn't. The traditional theological term for such action is 'sins of commission.' We will ourselves to dishonor God and rebel against His will. But the Scripture goes much deeper than merely addressing our actions. The Scripture teaches us that sin does not only lie in rebellion. It's in all we do, sadly. In other words, it's not that once in a while, we 'mess up' and break stuff. It's that we have a sinful mind, heart, and will. Sin is outside us, yes; but even more significantly, it's *inside* us. We've heard the spoiler of murder mysteries: the killer is calling from inside the house! In the case of our sin, we could say it this way: the evil man is calling from inside the heart.[1]

The Bible's most striking passage on this reality is James 1:13-15. In these few verses, James gives us a cardiology of the soul, showing us that we

---

1   We think of the economical yet piercing language of the *Westminster Shorter Catechism* here (Question 14): 'Sin is any want of conformity unto, or transgression of, the law of God.' This flows from the doctrine of total depravity, sketched in the prior chapter.

cannot necessarily pin temptation on others. Instead, we tempt ourselves:

> No one undergoing a trial should say, 'I am being tempted by God,' since God is not tempted by evil, and he himself doesn't tempt anyone. But each person is tempted when he is drawn away and enticed by his own evil desire. Then after desire has conceived, it gives birth to sin, and when sin is fully grown, it gives birth to death (James 1:13-15 csb).

This is a shocking look at how sin forms. It reverses ordinary thinking about wrongdoing. Many of us, caught out in something bad, would instinctively point to some factor around us and say, 'That's why I did it!' According to James, when we're struggling, we'll point even to God Himself as the one who deserves blame. This is, after all, exactly what Adam did when confronted by God over his sin. 'The woman *you gave* to be with me ...' Adam blamed his wife for eating the forbidden fruit, but he snuck in a still-greater dig at God. 'You made this woman,' he was saying in so many words, 'and so really blame sticks to you, God' (see Gen. 3:12).

James anticipates this wicked instinct. He cuts it no quarter. Sin is not a single isolated act. In biblical terms, sin comes from us. It does not come from God in any way – 'he himself doesn't tempt anyone,' period (v. 13). James locates our 'own evil desire' as the root of sin (v. 14). Led by a foul mind, our heart wants something wicked, something it should not want. We feel this, perhaps, in a flash, in an instant. We then let ourselves linger on this wicked matter (whether an image, thought, word, or anything else). We mull it over in our minds, thus allowing sin to come to term. Such sin will recur in patterns as we repeatedly allow ourselves to chase our 'evil desire' in our mind and heart, and this will in turn produce 'fully grown' evil that is a living state of 'death'. The language used here of a single sin is that of the implantation, nurture, and eventual birth of a single sinful deed. I suppose you could say this is a zombie birth story (admittedly a strange image). Truly, it is birth of a most terrible kind.[2]

As we can see, it is hard to underplay just how deep evil goes in us. This is what it means to have a sinful nature. Evil is not something external to

---

2   John Calvin helps us see that sin is found both in a definite action and in the desires that produce that action: 'It seems however improper and not according to the use of Scripture, to constrict the word sin to outward works, as though indeed lust itself were not a sin, and as though corrupt desires, remaining closed up within and suppressed, were not so many sins. But as the use of a word is various, there is nothing unreasonable if it be taken here, as in many other places, for actual sin.' John Calvin, *Commentary on James*, entry on James 1:15; accessible at http://www.studylight.org/commentaries/cal/view.cgi?bk=jas&ch=1. Last accessed January 2020.

us, the way many people think. Yes, there are murderers and thieves and sex-traffickers and cruel warlords in the world beyond us. You'll encounter many 'external' enticements to do wrong – commercials, pop-up ads, images, encouragement from peers, and much more. But the Bible teaches that each and every person has evil inside them. Our mind, heart, will, and soul are corrupted like software gone bad. Our operating system still works, but it does not work rightly. The product of our lives is not glorifying to God; instead, we produce sin, and sin produces death in us.

This is why people do bad things. They grow up in different settings, some of them peaceable, some of them tough. But even if they are raised in an idyllic setting, the happiest home imaginable, every person of every background has great capacity for wrongdoing. This is because to the core of our being, we are ruined. Sin has overtaken us like a terrible disease (see Rom. 3:10-18). But sin is *not* a disease, whether bodily or psychological. It's worse – it's our spiritual state and our personal nature. These words sound strange to modern ears, but when we sin, we're not doing something *abnormal* for us. When we sin, we're only doing what is *normal* per our condition. We're acting out who we really are. We're showing our true colors. We don't all sin in the same ways or to the same outward degree, but make no mistake, this is why we do bad things. We have fallen in Adam, and we are sinners by nature.

What About Jesus?

We should take a minute to clarify a couple matters. First, it is not wrong to find someone beautiful. The Bible introduces us to a number of figures who possess physical beauty: Rachel, Esther, and David to name a few (see Gen. 29:17, Esther 2:7, and 1 Sam. 16:18). Beauty is not bad in itself, though it must be stewarded carefully. Nor is it wrong to recognize God-given beauty in another person. There is more to say here, but the point is this: physical beauty is a gift from God, albeit one that pales in comparison to spiritual beauty (Prov. 31:30).

Second, the internal temptation we've discussed is a unique experience of people who have a fallen nature. Sometimes people think that Jesus experienced internal temptation, but this does not do justice to His divine identity. Yes, Jesus experienced the temptations presented to Him by Satan (Matt. 4:1-11). This was not a trifling prospect; Jesus had everything the human heart yearns for offered Him by Satan, but He resisted, and did so by the power of the Word. He was tempted like us in every way, and since He never yielded to temptation felt its force in full in a way we who yield to allurements do not (Heb. 4:15; see also 2:18).

But Jesus' surpassing temptation—covered in Hebrews—was the temptation of the cross. Drinking the wrath of His Father was unthinkable to the Son, yet He did it to the full.[3] This is because Jesus was the fully obedient Son of God in human form. He was the greater Adam, and like the first Adam, He had no sinful nature. He was *impeccable* (unable to sin). He was and is the true human, the one who shows us what it means to live for God with the fullness of heart, soul, mind, and strength in fulfillment of the first and greatest commandment (Matt. 22:37).

Jesus lived fully as a human being. He was not only human; he was *truly* human. But being human as God intended us to live does not involve sinning. Sin is a corruption of humanity; it is not an integral part of us. Though we all have a sinful nature, Jesus did not. Jesus was tempted in many ways, but He never had a lustful thought, an untoward desire, an evil passion. He was God in human flesh. There is no tension between the two natures of

3   See Denny Burk and Heath Lambert, *Transforming Homosexuality: What the Bible Says about Sexual Orientation and Change* (Phillipsburg, New Jersey: P&R, 2015), pp. 48-54.

Christ the person, for the natures 'communicate' to one another, though always in the direction we have just described. God cannot sin. God never has sinned, and never will sin (Hab. 1:13; Titus 1:2). This is an impossibility for God, and thus for the God-man.

Jesus thus shows us who we were meant to be, and what we will be when we go to God in heaven. His example calls us to overcome temptation, whether in our heart or from other people, and reminds us that by His life and death we have power over the flesh.[4] We note, then, that Jesus is like us, but also unlike us. We must get both right in order to do justice to Jesus and to His experience of temptation (and ours). If we overemphasize Jesus being like us, we will lose sight of the fundamental truth of His identity, His divinity. (Before His incarnation, Jesus exists eternally as the Son of God, after all, just as He does after it.) If we overemphasize Jesus being unlike us, we worship a docetic Christ, one who only seems human but is not.[5] In truth, we must take great pains to get the trajectory and chronology of the life of Christ right: eternally existent, He is God the Son in human form. He is the God-man. He is the

---

4   For more on this important and tricky point, see Denny Burk and Heath Lambert, *Transforming Homosexuality*.

5   'Docetic' comes from the Greek verb *dokeo*, which means 'to seem or appear.'

greater David, the greater Adam, the true Israel, the true Son, the promised Messiah, Immanuel.

We can say, then, that Jesus was like us, but also unlike us. He is not a *tertium quid*, a 'third thing,' but the true human as we have said above. He was the Son of God in human form. This means that He did not experience the temptation process described in James 1:13-15. He never faced internal temptation, and thus had no same-sex desires, no gender dysphoria, no bestial or pedophilic instincts, no sinful desire to kill anyone, and the like. There are two kinds of temptations presented in Scripture: external temptation and internal temptation. Jesus experienced the first but never the second (not even a hint). So we must take great care when we describe temptation in the life of Jesus, always taking into account His full humanity and His full divinity.

All this discussion positions us nicely to begin tackling the problem of lust. This is not a problem that is only external to us (though it definitely takes shape in unsought images, ads, scenes, presentation of body, and so on). If we are going to overcome lust, we are going to need to practice internal spiritual medicine. We must dig beneath the surface to identify our desires. This we do now by looking at biblical passages that warn against lust in both dimensions we've targeted in this book. We will now study Proverbs 7 in some detail, for it cautions the reader against lusting and wanting to be lusted after.[6]

The Wayward Man in Proverbs 7

The book of Proverbs is flush with wisdom. One of its most arresting methods is to pit the voice of wisdom against the call of the flesh. We see this method in Proverbs 7. This chapter is framed by a godly father speaking to his son. He has a specific mission he is communicating to his boy. He wants him to love the commandments of God. He wants him to befriend the truth. He wants him to do what is right. But his call is not vague; it has sharpness to it. This father, writing thousands of years ago, desires that his son would steer clear of 'the forbidden woman' (v. 5). This is no hint of sexism; Proverbs 31 praises a godly woman in lofty prose and lavish detail. No, the father in question has a temptress in mind. She is a hunter, and she wants sexual prey.

---

6   Some parts of this section are an expansion of an article I wrote. See Owen Strachan, 'Did Jesus Experience Same-Sex Attraction,' Center for Public Theology, September 4, 2019, accessible at https://cpt.mbts.edu/2019/09/04/did-jesus-experience-same-sex-attraction. Last accessed January 2020. Also see Reenchanting Humanity, Chapter 9, on Christological anthropology.

The father speaks from experience. He has watched, from his home, a certain kind of young man, 'a young man lacking sense' (v. 7). We do not hear him saying that this individual is in a neutral state; his senselessness is an indictment. This young man is not living wisely, cautiously, and righteously. He is instead wandering toward a bad situation, for he is walking near the forbidden woman's house. He is doing so 'in the twilight, in the evening, at the time of night and darkness' (v. 9). He should be at home; he should be resting up for the next day; he should be saying his prayers, and trusting the Lord. But he is doing none of these things. He is without sense, and he is in some way hoping that trouble will find him.[7]

Trouble does find him. An adulterous woman steps into the picture, 'wily' and alluring (v. 10). The text indicates this woman is seemingly everywhere, depicting the seriousness of the temptation young men face. The father wants his son to see that this mythical woman is not only found in a single home, but is an ever-present danger (vv. 11-12). She 'lies in wait,' in fact (v. 12). She's hungry for senseless youths. Derek Kidner says it well: 'Outwardly, she keeps nothing

---

7   This account in Proverbs 7 thus indicts both the sense-less youth and the temptress, not one or the other.

back; she is dressed, as we say, to kill; inwardly, she gives nothing away (v. 10b, lit. 'guarded of heart', meaning either hard, unyielding, or close, secretive). It will be an unequal contest.'[8] She has made a show of religiousness, but is not genuinely interested in God (v. 14). Her husband is away, she is sexually brazen and has readied her home with allurements, and she wants to drink her 'fill of love till morning' (v. 18).

We know the story here; we know the outcome, awful as it is. The young man follows this persuasion, this seemingly elegant seduction. He is transfixed by it, hungry for it, and oblivious to its costs. The father narrating this episode does not hold back; the young man complies with his tempter:

> as an ox goes to the slaughter,
>> or as a stag is caught fast
>> till an arrow pierces its liver;
>> as a bird rushes into a snare;
> he does not know that it will cost him his life.

The young man loses his life over this encounter, showing us that this is no mere physical happening. Sex—with lust fueling it—is spiritual. It is not a simple personal act. Sex is given by God for a married couple, but when pursued out of those

---

8   Kidner, *Proverbs*, Tyndale Old Testament Commentary (Downers Grove: Illinois, 2009), p. 71.

bounds is nothing less than 'slaughter' for the soul (v. 22). Ungodly sex involves ungodly spirituality which leads to destruction. There is no pure 'physical act,' as we so often hear today – 'Sex is just what I do with my body, it doesn't mean anything more.' This passage reminds us that sex is spiritual, linking people together in some hard-to-define way, and so we must approach sex with a pure heart and a pure body. The stakes are very high here.

The father concludes his story by making the point plain: 'Let not your heart turn aside to her ways,' he pleads with his son (v. 25). This particular tableau is fictional but grounded in reality. Many have gone to 'Sheol,' the realm of the dead, because of sexual sin (vv. 26-27). This chapter of Proverbs is not ultimately about which street you take when visiting a city. This is about the 'heart' as verse 25 reveals. The boy who is making his way into the world does not only need some practical tips and tools by which to avoid adultery or sexual sin more generally. The boy, this well-loved son, needs to watch his heart. His heart is the fullness of the matter. Do you love God, or do you love sin, the father is asking? Will you listen to wisdom (who calls aloud in Proverbs 8 as a counter-voice, the true voice), or will you listen to falsehood? Will you be ruled by lust, or will you rule lust?

If we think hard about Proverbs 7, we see that it addresses both forms of lust we have covered in this chapter (and book). The senseless young man seeks trouble—or rather all but asks trouble to seek him—and finds it. He is not careful with his heart; he does not watch his desires, and confess sinful ones and repent of them. Instead, he is careless with his heart, and allows his passion for sex outside of marriage to drive his choices. At some level, he wants the woman to find him; he wants an opportunity to act on his lust; accordingly, he does not want to listen to his godly father. He follows a false promise all the way to a temptress's bed, believing that his choice will bring the happiness he yearns to find. But it does not. The implication of the chapter is that the young man walks this road not once, but over and over and over, all the way into the realm of the dead.

The Wayward Woman in Proverbs 7

As we have seen, the senseless man desires rather vaguely to be tempted. He wanders in the general direction of temptation. That's one struggle we face regarding our sin. On the other side, we learn in this chapter about the sinfulness of wanting to tempt others. The young man pursues his lusts; the woman wants the attention and interest of a man who is not her husband. Proverbs 7 gives us these archetypes in order to warn us all about these traps. Yet we do not miss what the Scripture places before us. The wicked woman seeks sexual desire that is not hers to seek. She is no victim in the story. She wants to be wanted.

In Proverbs 7, we are not reading about a woman who goes about her business, seeks to be modest, and yet still has men yearn for her sexually. Women, to make the point as clear as we can, cannot finally control what others think of them. No mere human being—man or woman alike—will stand before God in light of the sins of anyone else. In terms of our approach to modesty, Scripture does not ask us to mask ourselves in plastic bags or never talk with others; it calls us to the continual pursuit of humility, including humility in dress, appearance, and demeanor. Modesty has great power, in reality, but it cannot necessarily repel all lust. We should never expect that it will, nor hold modest individuals guilty for the unrighteousness of others.

The Proverbs 7 woman, however, is not a careful, humble sort of individual. She puts herself out there in an aggressively forward way, making herself unmissable (vv. 11-12). She uses speech and immodest dress, the clothing of a 'prostitute' (v. 10). As much as things change over millennia, things really do stay the same. The young man clearly has a very strong interest in sex; the young woman clearly has a very strong interest in being wanted. She wants to gratify her lusts, and cares nothing for the young man (or her husband).[9] She clothes herself in such a way that the intentions of her heart are plain. Just as he is hoping that sin will find him, so she is hoping that sin will find her. She is not pursuing modesty at all; she is not keeping her heart carefully; she wants a man and uses all her person, all her sexual power, to get him.

Both of these people make numerous behavioral decisions that are at best unwise and at worst ungodly. Their decisions flow from their internal conditions. The young man is full of lust and interested in acting on it. The woman has a husband but wants someone else, seeking interest from a random young man. Proverbs 7 thus portrays for us in vivid form what James 1 reveals: it may take us a little while to express the fullness of our sinful longings, but we will do so regardless. We may need to make numerous decisions for our sin to come to full bloom, but such evil never happens by accident. We have a sinful nature, and so whether we act immorally in

---

9   See Waltke, *Proverbs*, pp. 374-78. To be clear on this point, both the man and the woman in this passage are giving into sexual desires. They are driven by their lusts.

a flash or in a pre-planned chain of activity, we will always act according to our nature.

But How Do I Know When I've Desired the Wrong Thing?

Our prayer is that you make the sad but very important discovery about the truth of lust. It's an external problem as we all know, but most significantly it's a problem of the heart. We don't need to change our behavior first and foremost; we need God to change our heart. This sounds well and good. But how do we know when we've desired something bad, as opposed to living innocently in a world that tempts us in many ways? In the New Testament, Jesus gives us the clarity we need. Matthew 5:27-30 answers this good question precisely:

> You have heard that it was said, 'You shall not commit adultery.' But I say to you that everyone who looks at a woman with lustful intent has already committed adultery with her in his heart. If your right eye causes you to sin, tear it out and throw it away. For it is better that you lose one of your members than that your whole body be thrown into hell. And if your right hand causes you to sin, cut it off and throw it away. For it is better that you lose one of your members than that your whole body go into hell.

Jesus here addresses the old covenant standard of holiness, referencing the seventh commandment. He affirms the principle, but expands on it. The act of committing adultery is wrong, yes, but so is looking at a woman 'with lustful intent' (v. 28). Here is a teaching that is sharp as a cutting diamond.[10] Whenever we lust after a member of the opposite sex who is not our spouse, we sin. In this context, a man who sexually desires a woman who is not his wife has committed adultery already 'in his heart' (v. 28).

Some may wonder, though, if there is a distinction between a quick burst of lust and a longer contemplation of adultery. Does the phrase 'with lustful intent' allow for a distinction between what we could call 'fallen internal temptation' and 'sinful internal temptation,' in other words? In short, we can make no such distinction. Any lustful experience, look, thought, desire, or act calls for repentance on our part. Lust, we see once more, is an issue of the heart.

---

10 D. A. Carson identifies the lustful desire condemned here: it is a 'deep-seated lust which consumes and devours, which in imagination attacks and rapes, which mentally contemplates and commits adultery.' Carson, *Jesus' Sermon on the Mount and His Confrontation with the World: An Exposition of Matthew 5-10* (Grand Rapids: Baker, 2004), p. 46.

The standard by which we know our desire is wrong is not the *duration* of the desire. It is wrong to look at a woman with lustful intent for two seconds, or eight seconds, or five minutes. The standard by which we know our desire is wrong is also not the *intensity* of the desire. It is wrong to look at a woman with lustful intent whether this sensation is an electric current running through us or a lesser wattage. The standard by which we know our desire is wrong is simply this: is the *end* we desire righteous or unrighteous?

It seems clear that the actual distinction Jesus is making is between lust and awareness. It is not wrong, for example, to identify a man or woman as beautiful. The Bible itself does this. We can meet a member of the opposite sex (for our purposes in this book) and note their God-given beauty, and this is not wrong. What is wrong, though, is to lust after such a person, to desire them sexually. This is precisely what Jesus is forbidding. In such circumstances (which apply, sadly, to us all), we want something we should not want. We may only rightly desire our spouse sexually; anyone else is off limits as per Matthew 5:27-30.

As we have said, then, what makes our desires worthy of confession and repentance is their goal, their end, their focus. If bestiality is wrong, it is wrong to desire it in any way for any length of time. If pedophilia is wrong, it is wrong to desire it in any way for any length of time. If coveting someone's stuff is wrong, it is wrong to desire those things in any way for any length of time. We could go on, but the point should be plain: *there is no good way to desire bad things.*[11] There is no righteous way to lust after someone who is not our spouse. We can note that a person is beautiful; we cannot allow ourselves even the merest contemplation of desire for them, however.

A Very High Standard

If it is sin to do it, it is sin to desire it. Desiring bad things is always wrong, always worthy of confession, always worthy of full-throated repentance before the Lord. Someone might say at this point,

---

11 Sometimes in this discussion, people point out that desires can be good or bad in Scripture. This is true – see Luke 22:15; Phil. 1:23; 1 Thess. 2:17; Rev. 18:14 for instances of positive uses, and Mark 4:19; Rom. 7:7; Col. 3:5; James 1:14; 2 Pet. 1:4 for instances of negative uses. But note carefully the teleological focus of the word. 'There are also bad ways to desire good things—which renders the desire itself bad. A misshapen desire for something seemingly good means that the desire is not right. The father who browbeats his son out of supposed "love" for him is not actually loving him, despite what he might say; he is sinning against him, and is acting without love.' See Burk and Lambert, *Transforming Homosexuality*, p. 52.

'But this seems like an awfully high threshold! Won't people who take Jesus seriously end up doing a lot of repentance?' Our response is this: great question, and you're entirely right! We remember here the teaching of Martin Luther: the whole of the Christian life is a life of repentance.[12] In other words, repentance isn't an occasional reality for born-again believers. Repentance is the doorway through which we enter the kingdom of Christ, and repentance is the drumbeat of the Christian life. Carson says it well: 'we are to deal drastically with sin. We must not pamper it, flirt with it, enjoy nibbling a little of it around the edges.'[13] No half-measures here: 'We are to hate it, crush it, dig it out,' Carson concludes.

Genuine Christianity, as we can see, looks like a whole lot of repenting. It is not a self-esteem project. It is a daily death to self. It involves the continual identification of lust and any evil desire. It entails confession and repentance, over and over again. But as we shall see, this is not

---

12 This is in fact the first of Luther's famous 95 theses: 'When our Lord and Master Jesus Christ said, "Repent" [Matt. 4:17], he willed the entire life of believers to be one of repentance.' Martin Luther, *Luther's Works: Career of the Reformer I*, Vol. 31, ed. Harold J. Grimm, Helmut T. Lehmann (Fortress, 1957), p. 25.

13 D. A. Carson, *The Sermon on the Mount: An Exposition of Matthew 5-7* (Carlisle, UK: Paternoster, 1994), p. 49.

spiritual defeatism for people who weirdly enjoy feeling bad about themselves. Disciplining ourselves by the Spirit's power is actually what triumph looks like.

In sum, Jesus gives us a high standard – a very high one. A heavenly one. He speaks to us the same wisdom that James and the righteous father of Proverbs 7 offer us. Together, these voices call us to flee what several passages in the New Testament call our 'evil lusts' (Col. 3:1-11; Titus 2:12). This is a strongly counter-cultural word today, but it is a vital one. It is the difference between spiritual life and spiritual death.

Conclusion

Our main goal in this chapter has been to show that defeating lust must be something more than replacing bad habits with good ones. We're all for good habits, but we need something stronger in us than mere behavioral change. Lust, as we saw throughout this chapter, is a viper. Lust will kill us. Our internal temptations, James teaches, produce death. Following the siren song of the temptress—and being the temptress herself—leads to Sheol, the realm of the dead. Failing to reckon with 'lustful intent' of the heart, Jesus proclaimed, means suffering in hell. All three biblical voices we have cited agree: when it comes to the lusts of the heart, the stakes could not be higher.

It is right when we are tempted to lust, or to be lusted after, to change up what we're doing. But too many Christians merely reshuffle the spiritual deck with regard to their sin. They take some action, that is, but they don't get to the heart of the matter. The Scripture has something far more powerful to offer us than a set of tips and helpful practices. The Scripture calls us to defeat sin at the level of desire, not merely the level of deed. Lust is not only a wayward decision; lust springs from a mind that thinks wrongly and thus a heart that wants evil ends.

Praise God, there is a stronger force in the cosmos than sin. Christ's mercy and grace are available to us; Christ is near to us. We have covered the 'bad news' of our depravity. Now we turn our attention to the 'good news,' the hope of the gospel.

3. CHRIST IS POWERFUL

I once asked one of England's top football managers (soccer coaches), 'What is the leadership key to gaining victory when the opposition is winning the game?' He answered, 'It is the ability to be like a surgeon and (i) see the problem, (ii) how bad it is and (iii) where it is on the field and then (iv) make the appropriate and effective change to solve the problem and make a successful outcome.' We need that kind of attitude to the issue of lust. We need, as the great coach said, to be like surgeons – spiritual surgeons. We need to identify the *problem*, its *scope*, its *location* and its *solution*.

We have already seen in Chapters 1 and 2 that sin is our great problem. And people are struggling with lust, because we live in a fallen world with our sinful desires. The problem of this human depravity means that although we are not as sinful as we could be in terms of degree, every part of us is affected by sin. A sinful heart taints the whole man or woman. That is its scope. Owen unpacked the Scriptures for us to reveal the heart as the location of lust in Chapter 2. He showed how lust is formed in the heart (powered by wrong thinking). The point is Satan can *tempt* us to sin, and in that sense has great effect, but he cannot *make* us sin. Sin corrupts the human mind and thus indwells the human heart and we actually tempt ourselves with our own lustful desire (James 1:13-15). Therefore, sinful sexual lust is a heart disorder—a desire disorder—a consequence of the fall, but something for which we are responsible.

So now we know what the problem is: sin. And lust is sinful sexual desire. We also know sin affects our whole person. That's the scope of the problem. We also see where it is located: the human heart. Our actions flow from our hearts. And that means *you* make *you* sin. This is the diagnosis of a faithful spiritual surgeon.

We have wrongly located and underestimated the problem

Because we have too often located lust as an outward action rather than an inward desire, we have underestimated the power of Satan and sin. We have fundamentally misunderstood how temptation and sin work. The culture around us with its normalization and moralization of sexual sin only helps to anesthetize us to the depth of its destructive power. Slowly, Satan begins to build a stronghold—a pseudo-reality—whispering lofty pretensions and lies, 'It's okay. Did God really say you're that sinful? Don't repent at every wrong sexual desire, you'll only be discouraged and despair of yourself. Only repent if you act upon the sinful desire. So go on, taste the fruit, just don't swallow it.'

Because we underestimate the power of sin and Satan, we do not realize the power we need to overcome the problem. Perhaps there has never been a time when sexual lust was more prevalent in culture and the visible church. But we often meet the problem with an inefficient solution. We try accountability programs, or accountability relationships, or we practice 'bouncing eyes,' or we simply try *really hard* not to follow through on lustful desires. All of this might appear to have some success on the surface of holding things back. But here is the reality: these efforts won't and can't kill the problem. This is true even if we say that Christ is the solution to the problem.[1]

---

1 Some evangelicals in our time rightly esteem Christ as our power for godliness, but their message seems to be, effectively, 'Look to Christ, for he did it all for you. You can't do anything; he did it all.' This is not untrue in terms of the passive and active righteousness of Christ. Yet we must take special care to distinguish between justification and sanctification. Our sanctification

Christ is the solution to the problem, yes, but if we are not watchful for Satan and if we don't think we are desperately sinful, we have under-realized the power of Christ, and have not appropriated His cruciform power at the root of sin.

In this chapter we will simply say that the solution to the problem of lust is found in the gospel of Jesus Christ. But Christ effects a powerful change in a person that transforms a life from defeat to victory (remember what the football manager said when speaking about the solution). We will see that the gospel of Christ results in transformation of the whole person.

Union with Christ

The great Scottish theologian, John Murray, once wrote that 'union with Christ is … the central truth of the whole doctrine of salvation. … It is not simply a phase of the application of redemption; it underlies every aspect of redemption.'[2] How needful this is. In this seminal passage, Murray taught that we don't just need a change

---

proceeds from Christ's finished work, applied to us by the Spirit. Sanctification is all of grace, but it involves real effort and considerable hard work, as this chapter—and book—argue.

2   John Murray, *Redemption Accomplished and Applied* (Eerdmans, 1955), pp. 201, 205.

of behavior. We need a change of heart desire because, as we have seen, the heart is the location of the sin problem in every person and the heart is the desire engine of the soul. Once we have a new heart we actually have the ability to produce sinless desires. All this happens when we are born again 'in Christ' by faith. So the gospel reality of our union with the person of Jesus Christ underpins our whole Christian life and is the foundation for mortification of lust.

We do not advocate sinless perfection in this life. This is abundantly clear in the New Testament (see 1 John 1). But we do advocate, as the Bible does, that the gospel is more powerful than we think and even though we may battle sinful, lustful desire all of our lives we can have increased victory in this life because we are united to Christ by faith. It is through union with Jesus Christ that we find true fulfillment and a new identity from which we find the power to overcome sinful lust and defeat Satan's temptations. So in Christ alone we find the complete resource we need to kill lust.

Nine realities of union with Christ

To win the fight against lust, we need to look at the power of being united to Christ. In Colossians, Chapters 2 and 3, notice the amount of times Paul uses the phrase 'in him' or 'with him'. He is driving us to see that the solution to our problem of sin and Satan can only be found in Christ. So Christ is the power that solves the problem of lust. Anything else will fall short. This is the Bible's testimony in Colossians 2:9-15.

> For in him the whole fullness of deity dwells bodily, and you have been filled in him, who is the head of all rule and authority. In him also you were circumcised with a circumcision made without hands, by putting off the body of the flesh, by the circumcision of Christ, having been buried with him in baptism, in which you were also raised with him through faith in the powerful working of God, who raised him from the dead. And you, who were dead in your trespasses and the uncircumcision of your flesh, God made alive together with him, having forgiven us all our trespasses, by cancelling the record of debt that stood against us with its legal demands. This he set aside, nailing it to the cross. He disarmed the rulers and authorities and put them to open shame, by triumphing over them in him.

To best understand how the gospel remakes us, we'll unpack this passage. In rapid-fire fashion, let's consider together nine transformative realities of being found in Christ. I'll list a verse or part of a verse and then offer comment on it.

(i) In Christ is Godness (Col. 2:9)

'For in him the whole fullness of deity dwells bodily...'

Jesus is the God-man. In Chapter 1 of Colossians Paul expands on the incarnate Jesus in rapturous prose: 'He is the image of the invisible God, the firstborn of all creation' (Col. 1:15). He is the image of God, fully God, equal to God, eternally existing with God. As John says, 'In the beginning was the Word, and the Word was with God, and the Word was God. He was in the beginning with God' (John 1:1-2).

You can go to extremes in many things, even good things. But you can never come to the end of the divinity, the awesomeness, of Jesus. Jesus, the God-man, who walked, talked, ate, slept, healed and wept on this earth is preeminent, above all and before all. Your mind will never exhaust Him nor will it ever find more power in anything or anyone else. Paul shows us this creation power in Colossians 1:16 when he says, 'For by him all things were created, in heaven and on earth, visible and invisible, whether thrones or dominions or rulers or authorities – all things were created through him and for him.' Paul communicates here that Christ is the agent of creation. Per the Father's appointment, all things were brought into existence by Him. The universe and all that is in it was not, until He commanded it to be. And His work is not local and limited or bound by earth. The sweep of His work surrounds the universe— the 200 billion plus galaxies—'heaven and earth.' It's His! He created it all. He owns it all.

John Eadie makes comment on this: 'Every form and kind of matter; simple or complex; the atom and the star, the sun and the clod; every grace of life from the worm to the angel; every order of intellect and being around and above us; the splendors of the heavens and the nearer phenomena of the earth are the product of the First Born.'[3] As Eadie argues, Christ not only creates and owns what exists within our line of vision but also what exists beyond it. The billions of stars and galaxies that we can see are a mere section of the stretch of fabric that is the universe that Christ made. And the further man penetrates into space even with the elastic eye of the Hubble telescope the stars are not dimmer nor scarcer, but new stars and new galaxies are bursting forth. Christ did this. This is important because we need to understand who He is *before* His incarnation before we can comprehend the

---

3   John Eadie: *Commentary on the Greek Text of the Epistle of Paul to The Colossians* (Robert Carter and Brothers, N.Y., 1856), p. 53.

power of the incarnate Christ in His crucifixion and resurrection.

Christ made and is supreme over everything on earth and in the heavens including fallen Satan and his minions and all the seraphim and cherubim; including all kings and rulers on earthly thrones. He controls empires about which we know nothing, and yet all pale to insignificance next to the Son of God. Any creature in the fullness of its glory is nothing compared to our Lord. No one is over Him; He is over everything because He has all authority.

Man, male and female, created in the image of God exists for Him. So He is the source and also the goal of it all! This means that our sexuality is made to serve Christ. It means, by extension, that we see in the very first pages of Scripture that sexual desire is fashioned for the one flesh covenant union of marriage between one man and one woman alone. Sexual desire in God's design cannot be severed or separated from God's plan for marriage to yield joy, fruitfulness and multiplication (Gen. 1:27-28; Gen. 2:23-24). Whatever we do in sexual terms must serve and honor Christ because He is God.

(ii) In Christ is fullness (Col. 2:10)

'... and you have been filled in him, who is the head of all rule and authority.'

If Christ is fully God and we are 'in Christ,' then through this union we have all we need. We don't need to go outside of Jesus for fulfillment of our pleasures. We don't need Jesus plus sinful lust for satisfaction. No, 'you have been filled in him.' There is nothing to add to this filling; it is complete, total, and final. We need nothing more than Christ. Being 'in him' we amazingly share in His power also. It says He is the 'head of all rule and authority.' Christ has authority over lust, and in Christ, so do you. Lust does not rule you any more.

(iii) In Christ is separation (Col. 2: 11)

'In him also you were circumcised with a circumcision made without hands, by putting off the body of the flesh, by the circumcision of Christ ...'

In Christ and by Christ there is a cutting away, a separation, from our fleshly life and a transferral to His lordship. We have new hearts that have been removed from Adam and sin and are now in union with Christ and righteousness, able to live for Him. This is a powerful realization for someone dealing with lust.

(iv) In Christ is new identity (Col. 2:12)

'... having been buried with him in baptism, in which you were also raised with him through faith in the powerful working of God, who raised him from the dead.'

This brings to light the fact that we are now with Christ in His death and resurrection. This is what baptism symbolizes: a dying to sin and rising to new life in Christ. Christ is where our identity lies now. Though we still sin, sin does not define us. Sin lies in the depths of the baptismal water. Now, you are not a 'lustful Christian.' You are a Christian. You may be a Christian who has lusted. But Christ defines you, not lust.

(v) In Christ is life (Col. 2:13)

'And you, who were dead in your trespasses and the uncircumcision of your flesh, God made alive together with him ...'

Only in Christ is there true spiritual life. Outside of Christ we are dead in sins. This means that lust is the work of the flesh – a dead work. It has nothing to do with Christ or the Christian united to and set apart in Christ. It is a corruption of goodness, not a positive substance. Though it threatened to kill us, in Christ we are made alive.

(vi) In Christ is forgiveness (Col. 2:13)

'... having forgiven us all our trespasses'

This is the amazing power of life-giving grace. Forgiveness of sins is found in Christ. And note 'all our sins' are forgiven in Christ: sins from the past, present and future. So in Christ the sin of lust, every lustful impulse, is forgiven. How? We see in the next verse.

(vii) In Christ is victory over Satan and sin. (Col. 2:14-15)

'... by cancelling the record of debt that stood against us with its legal demands. This he set aside, nailing it to the cross. He disarmed the rulers and authorities and put them to open shame, by triumphing over them in him.'

Let us dwell on these verses a little. Paul teaches us that there is a divine record of the debt of our lust. This record counts against us. The debt we have is twofold: (a) Lust means we do not legally fulfill God's holy just law and (b) lust means we legally warrant punishment for that crime. We have a demand we cannot meet and a punishment we cannot bear. So what does God do?

This twofold debt He set aside, nailing it to the cross. The record of debt is pounded into the hands and feet of Jesus. Every person who has lusted and then who repents and trusts in Christ can look up at that cross and see that his or her sexual sin was borne by Christ, who became a curse on behalf of them, was pierced for their transgressions, and exhausted the just wrath of

God poured out upon Him instead of them. Jesus meets the twofold debt by (a) perfectly fulfilling the demands of God's law because He never sinned, including the sin of lust, and (b) meeting the demand of God's justice by absorbing the punishment for sin, including the sin of lust, in the place of whoever trusts in Him. The twofold debt is paid. Sin is defeated at the cross.

How we need this truth to fight against our foe, Satan. Satan loves to taunt us with our guilt before God. Satan loves to tempt us with lustful pleasures of the mind and body. Satan loves to say to God as it were, 'Send them to Hell. They lusted; it's a sin against you and if you are a just God you must punish them. You say in your Word that the sexually immoral will not enter the kingdom. You can't go back on your Word. Punish them.' But God says to Satan, 'I did punish them. Look at my Son on the cross of Calvary, bleeding in their place, bearing their sin.'[4]

This is precisely where Paul drives us. He wants us to focus not on our guilt, but on Christ:

---

4   See Isaiah 53 on this count. For a crucial reference on the nature of the atonement, consult Steve Jeffrey, Michael Ovey, and Andrew Sach, *Pierced for Our Transgressions: Rediscovering the Glory of Penal Substitution* (Wheaton: Crossway, 2007). This is a masterful book on this contested doctrine, called penal substitutionary atonement.

'He [God] disarmed the rulers and authorities and put them to open shame, by triumphing over them in him [Christ].' Satan's only weapon against us is unforgiven sin, and Christ takes that away nailing it to the cross. By overcoming sin, Christ disarms Satan and triumphs over him. In Christ the power of Satan and sin is broken in your life. Its presence remains there but you are not enslaved anymore.[5] So where else will you go to deal with your lust? Only Christ is powerful enough to gain victory over the problem, its extent, and its location. Which makes Christ the only solution. The crucified Christ is the powerful solution, for He made atonement for sin and then rose from the grave, granting life to all who repent and believe.

(viii) In Christ is a new destiny (Col. 3:4)

'When Christ who is your life appears, then you also will appear with him in glory.'

---

5   This is a crucial matter of identity that sadly some are not getting quite right today. We *are* the new man, a new creation in Christ. While we are not the old man, the old man—our sinfulness—still pulls at us. It does not have power over us unless we grant it power. Getting our identity in Christ right is crucial to gaining victory over the flesh. We are not half-righteous, half-unrighteous; we are a new man who must nonetheless fight the pull of the old man every day we live.

Moving into chapter three we read that this union with Christ is such that when He returns He will bring all those 'in him' with Him. There are many things we will experience individually as Christians. But when He physically returns to glorify His people, we will experience this glorification together. That is the destiny for all Christians: the day when we will have glorified bodies with every trace of indwelling sin removed such that we will neither desire to sin nor be able to sin. Lust will be no more.

We must see that these eight realities found in Christ equip us to fight Satan and sin *now*. We don't wait until heaven to get holy. We don't carry on sinning saying, 'It doesn't matter because Jesus died for my sins.' We don't *let go and let God* saying, 'He will sanctify me. I don't need to do anything.' And, we don't say, 'This is just the way I was born. I cannot help it. This is something I just struggle with.'

No, if these eight realities are true for us because we have repented and been united to Christ by faith, then we cannot and must not remain the same. We are yoked to the One through whom the universe was made. That is awesome power that Christ exercised. It is this divine power, that Paul indicates in other places, that is at work in believers (Phil. 2:13). That is a sensational thought! 'God's power works in me. I have the Holy Spirit in me. Christ's life is my life,' we need to remind ourselves. Not for nothing did the Puritan Henry Scougal call this the 'life of God in the soul of Man.'[6] So it is: God's life is in us. What a marvel!

Scougal was not alone in this conviction. Another Puritan, Matthew Henry, says, 'Those that are born again are dead to sin, because its dominion is broken, its power gradually subdued by the operation of grace, and it shall at length be extinguished by the perfection of glory. To be dead, then, means this, that those who have the Holy Spirit, mortifying within them the lusts of the flesh, are able to despise earthly things, and to desire those that are heavenly.'[7] Note what Henry says here. Christians who have the Holy Spirit—this life of God in the soul—'are able to despise earthly things and to desire those that are heavenly.' This is a very hopeful truth for anyone stuck in lust, or anyone, like many Christians, who still experience lustful impulses. We are able to

---

6   See Henry Scougal, *The Life of God in the Soul of Man*, 1677.

7   Matthew Henry, *Concise Commentary on the Bible*, Colossians 3, accessible online at https://www.christianity.com/bible/commentary.php?com=mhc&b=51&c=3. Last accessed January 2020.

have new desires. Desire is not wrong; God is not trying to eradicate desire in us, or erase our feelings and passions. Not by a long shot!

No, it is the object or end of the desire that makes it right or wrong. Desire is not neutral, therefore. It is either good or bad. Denny Burk offers further clarification: 'The only time *epithumia* (desire) is good is when it is directed toward something morally praiseworthy. *Epithumia* is always evil when it is directed toward something morally blameworthy. Thus, desires either have their end in that which is heavenly or that which is earthly.'[8] This is exactly right. Desire isn't bad all the time; God wants us to have desire for that which is good. This is precisely what the Spirit births in us: zeal for God and His glory. But the Lord also wants us to make war on our evil desires. Praise God, we do not only fight; we may have victory over them. So here is a ninth reality of being in Christ.

(ix) In Christ is transformation and victory

You can't be abstract or general in your fight against sin. You've got to do targeted strikes. Consider what Puritan theologian John Owen says

8   Denny Burk, 'Is Temptation Sinful?,' July 11, 2018, accessible online at http://www.dennyburk.com/is-temptation-sinful. Last accessed January 2020.

on this count: 'To "mortify sin" is "to take away the principle of all [its] strength, vigor, and power, so that [it] cannot act or exert, or put forth any proper actings of [its] own.'[9] Owen is articulating what the Scripture powerfully teaches. See, for example, how Paul challenged the Colossian church to mortify sin. He began with a command to *seek* and *set*. In other words, desire things that are above and fix your minds on them:

> If then you have been raised with Christ, seek the things that are above, where Christ is, seated at the right hand of God. Set your minds on things that are above, not on things that are on earth. For you have died, and your life is hidden with Christ in God. When Christ who is your life appears, then you also will appear with him in glory (Col. 3:1-4).

Being in Christ means being empowered to do something. So *seek* and *set*. It is an intellectual, affectional, and wilful action. Realize—with everything in you—who you are in Christ. Notice Owen grounds this action in the indicative truth of the gospel: You are 'in Christ' in His death and resurrection and return. A simple and logical conclusion we must then draw is this: *only* a Christian can put sin (and

---

9   John Owen, *Works Volume Six: Temptation and Sin* (Banner of Truth, 2000), p. 8.

therefore lust) to death, because only someone united to Christ by faith has the power to do it.

However, Paul continues with even more specific instruction here: 'Put to death therefore what is earthly in you: sexual immorality, impurity, passion, evil desire, and covetousness, which is idolatry' (Col. 3: 5). Let me spell out a little further how we can honor and actualize this teaching.

Firstly, name the sin. So we must name lust – sexual immorality. Confess it in order to kill it. Don't be general. Admit what it is. It is 'earthly', Paul says. That is the opposite of heavenly. It is the opposite of what is true and good: it is a lie and it is evil. So not repenting of sexually immoral impulses, thoughts and actions, of any kind is embracing an earthly evil lie. Remember to repent at impulse level even if they are uninvited (see Owen's treatment of the formation of sin in Chapter 2).

But, *secondly*, go even deeper. Alongside sexual lust are other sins. For instance, porn promises power and respect: a man may not feel powerful in his work or home. He might not feel respected. So he buys the illusion of authority and respect in a porn world where he can have whomever and do whatever he wants. The idols of power and control lie under the sexual lust. These idols need to be killed.

Another thing porn promises is acceptance. You are always accepted in the fantasy world. A woman may try to medicate loneliness, a lack of intimacy and a sense of unworthiness with porn, or romance, or erotic fantasy novels. But underneath is the idol of acceptance and affirmation. She desires to be worshiped by men. The idol of acceptance and affirmation is what really drives her lust.

Porn also promises revenge. You are tired, you have been wronged, you feel you deserve better treatment, your wife doesn't want sex, you want to be married and the Lord hasn't provided yet, you lost your job. Your anger after disappointment finds its revenge in pornography. You didn't get what you wanted so you are doing porn because you deserve a denied pleasure and you want to feel immediately comforted. But really you are just acting out frustration against God. The idol of self-righteousness is driving your lust.[10]

Men and women will experience diverse motives that drive them to pornography. Whatever the specific motive that helps fuel lust—and raw pagan carnality regularly does—neither porn nor any sexual pursuit delivers on its promises. It feeds the idols and the idols control you. That's

---

10 This section is informed by Tim Chester and his work in *Captured by a Better Vision* (IVP, 2010), pp. 52-69.

what an addiction is. The key is to discover the idols beneath sexual immorality. As we saw above, John Owen called this 'detecting the flesh.'

Thirdly, consider the consequences of your lust. Think of this strong biblical word: 'On account of these the wrath of God is coming' (Col. 3:6). Think how much God hates lust. His wrath is coming because of it. Think how your lust harms people around you: spouse, children, friends. Think how watching porn fuels a whole industry, a web of child prostitution and enslavement of women and so on.

Wrath is coming for unbelievers which means if you are a believer, that click of the mouse button was a nail in Christ's hand as He absorbed wrath in your place, and even that impulse— however instantaneous and un–premeditated—is something that Christ hung for at Calvary. But as you consider the consequences make sure it is not legal guilt you feel but evangelical (gospel) guilt. Hear John Owen again:

> Bring thy lust to the gospel-not for relief [yet] but for farther conviction of its guilt ... Say to thy soul, 'What have I done? What love, what mercy, what blood, what grace have I despised and trampled on! Is this the return I make to the Father for his love, to the son for his blood, to the Holy Ghost for his grace? Do I thus requite the Lord? Have I defiled the heart that Christ died to wash, that

the blessed spirit has chosen to dwell in? ... Do I account communion with him of so little value, that for this vile lust's sake I have scarce left him any room in my heart? Shall I endeavor to disappoint the [purpose] of the death of Christ?' Entertain thy conscience daily with this treaty. See if it can stand before this aggravation of its guilt. If this make it not sink in some measure and melt, I fear thy case is dangerous.[11]

What wise words these are. They may sound strange to us today, accustomed as we all are to affirmation, positivity, and self-esteem culture. In fact, Owen may sound downright gloomy to some, a theological gloom-sayer. But he is not. Owen is showing us the way back to holiness in the wake of sin. We should not smile brightly when we lust and do wrong; we should take stock of just how serious our sin is, not blinking it away, not changing the subject, not allowing ourselves to escape so easily. Those who would make progress in the fight for holiness must be those who feel real guilt when they do wrong.

We cannot overstate the importance of such a practice, odd as it may appear today. Truly, Owen's aim should be our own: to kill desire for sexual immorality by making it lose attractiveness and

---

11 John Owen, *Temptation and Sin*, p. 58.

therefore disarming its power to excite us. We don't need superficial repentance. We need deep repentance. We don't need to move on too quickly from guilt to grace. This is a terrific temptation in a man-centered context like ours, unable as it so often is to face hard truth. But we should not hasten the work of conviction. We need to mourn our sin. 'Blessed are those who mourn,' Jesus said. Superficial repentance can be based on self-love rather than love for God: you are motivated by your fear of damage to your reputation. In similar terms, you might experience sorrow because you've been caught in sin rather than grieving that you've sinned against God and hurt people. If we are not careful, our repentance can be intellectual repentance rather than heart-level evangelical conviction.

Loading the conscience with appropriate 'evangelical guilt' is what makes us tear out an eye or cut off an arm as Jesus talks of in the Sermon on the Mount. That is what makes us violently and urgently put off sexual immorality and put it to death – and not stroke it and put it in a cage. So load the conscience with evangelical guilt of sin. Then, put on Christ. If all you do is put off you only do half the job of mortifying sin. Something else will fill the gap. Instead realize who you actually are: we are those by God's grace 'have put on the new self, which is being renewed in knowledge after the image of its creator.' (Col. 3:10). Notice that you have to put on the new self. It is done: past tense. And you are being renewed in the knowledge and image of the creator: present tense. It is happening. There is a past and present action of being in Christ. And there is a future ongoing action that is needed.

Consider the text in full:

> Put on then, as God's chosen ones, holy and beloved, compassionate hearts, kindness, humility, meekness, and patience, bearing with one another and, if one has a complaint against another, forgiving each other; as the Lord has forgiven you, so you also must forgive. And above all these put on love, which binds everything together in perfect harmony (Col. 3:12-14).

The Christian life is a life of repentance. That means a constant putting off and putting on whilst seeking and setting minds on things above.

One Man's True Story of Deliverance

The material we have covered thus far is not abstract. It is real. The gospel is real, and it really does change lives. In years of counseling, I (Gavin) have seen real change occur in those enslaved to their lusts. Here is one true story from an anonymous man helped by the doctrines sketched thus far in the book. I present it at length as a trophy not of our ingenuity, but of God's grace:

> Years before I first encountered porn (by accident, and soon after intentionally), I had become accustomed to objectifying and sexualizing women. I remember discussing women's physical appearance with other boys in my second grade class. I had a vague sense of shame regarding these conversations and thoughts. My father would often recite Scripture to my siblings and me, including the Sermon on the Mount from Matthew 5-7. I understood from this that Jesus is concerned not just with actions, but also thoughts, of lust, or anger, or fear. But at this point in my life, I was not yet a Christian, with the main barrier to belief being my own self-righteousness. So I suppressed the thoughts as best as I could and called it good enough.
>
> Later when I encountered porn in fifth grade, I had this framework of sinful desire ready to go and began to indulge habitually. I had recently professed faith, and I remember confessing my sin over and over in prayer and a few times to my father, but in my heart I didn't want to let go of my desires. I'm sad to say that this went on for twelve years. I was in my first year of graduate school and engaged to be married when I attended a conference for men held by my hometown church. Knowing that I was poised to make a mess of my upcoming marriage, I reluctantly attended a session focused on pornography.

I was shocked to see so many of the men attend, and even more shocked when a few men I greatly looked up to shared that they had been enslaved in the way that I was – and were now free! I had never considered that this was a sin I could be freed from; only that I might sin less often or more often. Wanting to be free from the consequences of the sin, but with more than a decade of porn use warping my conscience, I went home and followed the advice I got at the conference. I confessed to my dad (again), my local pastor, my fiancé, and even my employer, whose computer I had been using to access porn.

Exposing my sin in this way had a powerful effect on the way I viewed sexual immorality, allowing me to see it as truly damaging: my prayer life and interaction with Scripture were essentially non-existent, and my personal relationships, especially with women, were distorted. This exposure also gave me the first tool to help me successfully battle lust: other Christians.

o Tool #1. God does not intend us to be Christians in a vacuum, but that had been my posture in this sin for so long. When I confessed my sin to other believers, I learned that rather than being scornful, they were on my side, wanting to help me towards victory as much as I would let them. This confession and exposure became my first real tool for fighting my sin. And since then, various friends, family and pastors (Gavin Peacock being the most recent) have given me further tools with which to battle temptation.

o Tool #2: know that victory is possible: Paul tells us that it is a trustworthy saying 'that Christ Jesus came into the world to save sinners, of whom I am the foremost' (1 Tim. 1:15). If you feel like the foremost of sinners, you are not beyond the reach of Christ's sacrifice.

o Tool #3: recognize that sin starts with desire, and repent of the desire before it progresses. Before I ever viewed porn, I harboured lust in my heart. Now when I begin to fantasize, I recognize that desire as sin-to-repent-of before it progresses to action.

o Tool #4: recognize other sinful desires motivating the lust. I have sinful desires for ease, wealth, and lack of responsibility that, unchecked, lure me to the false promises of satisfaction and escape promised by porn. Repenting of these desires first often heads off subsequent lustful temptation.

o Tool #5: replace sinful desire. Without something else to yearn for, the human heart will always return to uprooted sin. Read the Bible. Memorize Scripture. Pray routinely. Regular time spent in the pursuit of God will only make

God more desirable. It's a positive feedback loop. You won't ever get enough of him.[12]

These tools have given me significant victory over lust in the past few years, though punctuated by instances of rebellion. Repentance is still very hard work, but it is work empowered by the Holy Spirit, and encouraged by the body of Christ around me. I have great hope.

Conclusion

We hope this beautiful testimony inspires and encourages you as it does us. What hope there is, we see, in embracing the whole-sidedness of the gospel. If we rightly diagnose the *problem* (its scope and its location), and if we have a right estimation of the power of Satan and sin, then we will realize that secular methods of counseling and rehab for lust and sexual addiction will not do. Only the *solution* found in Christ will do. Christ is a treasure chest of power and riches for the Christian. We often have too low a view of who He is and what He has achieved for us and who we are in Him. But when we lift our eyes to these glorious gospel truths and embrace them, and act upon them by

---

12 We requested this testimony, but did not shape or alter it in any way. Though anonymous, it is a real story of deliverance from sin.

faith, lust can be killed. This is what happened for the young man whose story we just encountered.

Lust is serious. This chapter has laid that out clearly: but the way we deal with it is the same way we deal with any sin: by embracing the grace and goodness and love and power of Jesus Christ. In the next chapter we will lay out some very practical steps that flow out of this chapter for how to fight lust and win.

4. WE HAVE HOPE

It would be a hopeless thing for a person who is stuck in lust to approach this book as a Christian if they are not. But it would be equally hopeless if you profess to be a Christian and carry on living in lust. To put it another way, as you look at Chapter 3 are you convinced you are united to Christ by faith? Are those nine realities in some way true for you?

By paraphrasing John Owen's words in *A Treatise on the Dominion of Sin and Grace*, Sinclair Ferguson has described the two main aims of pastoral ministry as: 'To convince those under sin's dominion that this is their predicament really. The second is to convince others that they are not.'[1] If you are that first person—the one under sin's dominion—then you need evangelizing. We urge and invite you to believe the nine gospel realities of Chapter 3 for the first time. You need new life

---

1 Sinclair Ferguson, *John Owen on the Christian Life* (Banner of Truth, 2001), p. 127.

– it is there before you! You need to be saved from the judgment of sin before you can engage in the mortification of sin. Your great hope is that 'everyone who calls on the name of the Lord will be saved' (Rom. 10:13). Then you will be united to Christ and those nine realities will be true for you. You will then have the power to kill your lust because your lust will not have dominion over you anymore. Our great hope is that even through this book you may find yourself in the category of that second person – one who is in Christ having trusted in Him for salvation.

If you are the second person—the one not under sin's dominion but in Christ already—you need to realize those nine realities are already true for you and live out of those truths. The great hope is that you have all you need in Christ already. So instead of trying to be what you are not, be who you are: You are not half-dead, half-alive; you have walked out of the grave like Lazarus. You are united to Christ. Sin's dominion is broken. 'We know that our old self was crucified with him in order that the body of sin might be brought to nothing, so that we would no longer be enslaved to sin. ... Let not sin therefore reign in your mortal body, to make you obey its passions' (Rom. 6:6,12). What a crucial word this is – one that will propel us onward in our fight against the flesh.

Eight Steps in the Battle Against Lust

Picture a young man or woman who has the talent to become a professional athlete. They also have the motivation. They know what the end goal looks like, and they have their mind and heart set on it. They understand the principles behind everything. But they just don't know how to practically get from being an amateur to being a professional. They need to be shown the practical steps: what it looks like on the ground.

It's like that with a Christian who wants to battle lust. And there are many in that category. They are not the people who say, 'It doesn't matter because Jesus died for my sins.' They don't *let go and let God* saying, 'He will sanctify me. I don't need to do anything.' They don't say, 'This is just the way I was born. I cannot help it. It's just something with which I personally struggle' (referred to in Chapter 3). No, they believe the nine realities of Colossians 2 and 3. They have made a start. But they just need more practical help in waging the war. What follows are eight steps to take in the battle against lust; eight steps, which are the outworking of being in Christ; our hope of transformation.

(i) Pursue accountability

I am always glad when a young man has come forth and confessed his lust and asked for help. Confession is key. Confession is the first response that results from conviction of sin (see 1 John 1:9). Maybe that conviction has happened as you've read this book. But confession doesn't always mean repentance, and repentance is what transforms us.[2] Repentance means that there is a change.

Finding a person to whom you will be accountable helps here. They hear your confession. Good. But they also help structure the way of repentance for you. A trusted accountability partner provides direction and correction but also safety and security and the knowledge that you are not alone. Feeling alone in a fight with a sin that can bring with it very shameful feelings can be very discouraging. An accountability partner can also bring perspective that the person in the sin cannot see (which is often *because* they are in sin). Like Nathan with David, a wise counselor can help a person realize sin of which they need to repent.

---

2   Repentance always goes hand in hand with saving faith. The two are not the same, but could be characterized as two sides of the same coin. Think of Mark 1:15, where Christ exclaims, 'The time is fulfilled, and the kingdom of God is at hand; repent and believe in the gospel.'

What does an accountability structure look like? In the case of the young man who comes to me, he needs to text message me once a week literally to say whether there have been instances of lust/porn watching. This provides an immediate discipline in his life: something that is clearly missing if he has a lust problem. It also provides us both with a logbook so he can hopefully see his progress in writing as the weeks go on. We also meet regularly face to face. In these sessions I try to help him see what sin may be beneath the sin (remember John Owen: 'detect the flesh'), understand his union with Christ and what that means, and show what repentance looks like. In all this I make it known that he can call me at any time, especially if he is feeling tempted.

Once a person has sought accountability the rest of this list is what we will work on. In practical terms, everything flows from accountability propelled by God's grace.

(ii) Understand the Christian view on sex and sexuality

We must set the mind on right biblical thinking. The New Testament writers all affirm God's creation design for heterosexual sex within the marriage covenant alone. Whether it is Paul speaking about marriage in Ephesians 5 or talking about sexual immorality in 1 Corinthians 6, he affirms Genesis 2:24 as his framework of reference.

Jesus affirms the same in Matthew 19:

> And Pharisees came up to him and tested him by asking, 'Is it lawful to divorce one's wife for any cause?' He answered, 'Have you not read that he who created them from the beginning made them male and female, and said, "Therefore a man shall leave his father and his mother and hold fast to his wife, and the two shall become one flesh"? So they are no longer two but one flesh. What therefore God has joined together, let not man separate' (Matt. 19:3-6).

We will briefly note three truths from Jesus' words here.

Firstly, Jesus' foundation for marriage and sexuality is God's Word at creation. The Pharisees are trying to trap Jesus. They 'tested him,' by asking a question on marriage and divorce. So Jesus appeals to God's Word at creation. He answers, 'Have you not read that he who created them from the beginning made them male and female?' Here Jesus quotes from some of the very first words in the Bible in Genesis 1:27 and the creation of the sexes. Jesus sets His sexual ethic in the Old Testament creation mandate.

Secondly, God created binary sexes. Note that Jesus says there are two sexes only: 'Have you not read that he who created them from the beginning made them *male and female*?' This is crucial for our identity and our thinking about right sexual desire.

Thirdly, God created complementary sexes to come together in marriage. Look at Genesis 1:27 again which Jesus refers to in Matthew 19: 'So God created man in his own image, in the image of God he created him; male and female he created them.' In that one statement, there is equality and difference. Although the man and woman are both made equally in the image of God, they are not the same. One is male and one is female. The careful reader will also understand that their physiques and functions flow out of their created sex. Directly after Genesis 1:27 God commands them to be fruitful and multiply.

After Jesus quotes Genesis 1:27 he quotes Genesis 2:24. He moves to marriage. Jesus says that God made man and woman for marriage as a creation ordinance. After the creation of woman God says, 'Therefore [because I made a man and woman] a man shall leave his father and his mother and hold fast to his wife and the two shall become one flesh.' God created binary, complementary sexes for the purpose of heterosexual union in the covenant of marriage in order to multiply imagers of God. This is Biology 101, friends. Nature and common sense tell us that it takes a human man and a human woman to make a human baby. It is obvious and cannot be changed. So at their point of most physical difference a man and woman can come together, become one flesh and create life. This is beautiful, wise design – divine, you could say.

Moreover, the fruit of this complementary male-female sexual union—a baby—means that only a man can become a father and only a woman can become a mother. That this sexual union is to take place within the covenant of marriage between a man and woman also means that only a man can be a husband and he is only a husband in reference to a woman who is his wife. And only a woman can be a wife and she is only that in reference to a man who is her husband. Both roles of husband and wife—with him as head and her as helper, with him as father and her as mother—are the immediate consequence of being made male or female in Genesis 1:27. We could sum it up by saying that sexual desire and function, and gender roles flow out of being made male or female.

Finally, the scriptures show us that the marriage of a man and a woman is meant to be a picture of the gospel, with husbands lovingly leading like Christ, and wives respecting and submitting to that headship like the church. The act of sexual consummation within this marriage joyfully affirms the truth and beauty of this spiritual picture.

As we have noted, the Bible begins with a marriage in Genesis (creation) and ends with a marriage in Revelation (consummation). It is not too strong to say that the central theme of the Scriptures is the marriage of the Bridegroom who came from heaven and sought His Bride the church (redemption). The Bible tells us the greatest love story in history. It gives us the greatest display of the love of the triune God. A trinity of self-existent love overflowing, as the Father loves the Son and bequeaths to Him a Bride, as the Son comes and accomplishes her purchase by dying for her on the cross, and as the Spirit applies that redemption to the hearts of the Bride for whom Christ dies.

All this, so that when Jesus returns for His Bride and takes us to himself forever all of heaven will sing, 'Let us rejoice and exult and give him the glory, for the marriage of the Lamb has come, and his Bride has made herself ready' (Rev. 19:7). Marriage and sex is not ultimate, then; the marriage of Christ and the Church is ultimate. Honorable as it is, this earthly picture will one day give way to the heavenly reality and forever we will sing of the glory of the crucified and risen Christ's covenant love for His Bride.

Furthermore, this glorious gospel that redeems us, then begins to re-order and conform our fallen desires to what is natural – beginning with complementary unity, and moving next to complementary polarity (distinctiveness) and then complementary reciprocity. Many will also find within themselves complementary interest and complementary desire for marriage. Owen unpacked this carefully for us in Chapter 1, duly noting that not all of us will be called to marriage and many of us will continue to fight remaining sinful, sexual lusts. All this means that being in Christ by faith doesn't eliminate or change God's creation design for sex and sexual desire which now serve redemption and consummation purposes. It affirms it, seeing it as inextricably bound with 'new creation' fulfillment.[3]

(iii) Preach the gospel to yourself regularly

Jerry Bridges sums up this daily practice well in his book *Respectable Sins*:

> Since the gospel is only for sinners, I begin each day with the realization that despite my being a saint, I still sin every day in thought, word, deed, and motive. If I am aware of any subtle, or not

---

3   As we have stated elsewhere, knowing these truths equips us for personal transformation. Without such knowledge of the truth, real transformation will not occur. How important is the knowledge of the truth, then (see Rom. 12:1-2).

so subtle, sins in my life, I acknowledge those to God. Even if my conscience is not indicting me for conscious sins, I still acknowledge to God that I have not even come close to loving Him with all my being or loving my neighbor as myself. I repent of those sins, and then I apply specific Scriptures that assure me of God's forgiveness to those sins I have just confessed. Maybe it's a verse like this: 'There is therefore now no condemnation for those who are in Christ Jesus (Rom. 8:1).[4]

This is a vital daily practice. But I also advocate preaching the gospel to yourself in the *moment of temptation*. Consider this: It's late at night. You are tired, discouraged, angry, lonely or all of these things. A thought comes into your mind that if you click a button on your device you can see images or video that will bring you sexual pleasure. Maybe you have already begun to lust in your heart. Satan is whispering in your ear, as it were, saying, 'Go on. You've already sinned. You might as well go all the way.' In *that moment* you preach the gospel to yourself, saying 'I am not that person anymore. Christ died for that sin. He died for the sin I am about to commit. And he died for the sin I have already committed. I died in Christ. So I have died

4   Jerry Bridges, *Respectable Sins: Confronting the Sins We Tolerate* (Colorado Springs, Colorado: NavPress, 2007), pp. 37-38.

121

to sin. I am united to Jesus not Adam. And Jesus promises never to leave me nor forsake me until I get to heaven.'

In that moment you turn away from the fleeting promise of sin to the gospel promise of Christ. This is what victory looks like – victory in Jesus. I got the chance to be a part of winning many football matches (soccer games) in England. I still remember the victories. The feeling was thrilling. But nothing—nothing at all—compares to the victory we experience daily in Christ.

(iv) Pray regularly

I do a good bit of pastoral counseling and have for some time now. Anyone whom I have ever counseled for an issue with lust had an issue with prayer. They were not doing it regularly. Their prayer life was sparse so they were not watchful of sin. No doubt this is an area of weakness for most of us. You would think we would spot this easily, but we all tend to forget how closely linked defeated faith and prayerlessness truly are.

Remember how Jesus counsels his disciples: 'Watch and pray that you may not enter into temptation. The spirit indeed is willing, but the flesh is weak' (Matt. 26:41). But mark what happened next: the disciples fell asleep and it wasn't long before Peter was being rebuked for cutting off the ear of the servant of the high priest, and then denying Jesus three times.

We must develop daily prayer times in order to cultivate a powerful sense of the realities of Chapter 3 – our union with Christ. In those prayer times we can also ask Him for help in moments of temptation. By employing this advice my wife has helped many young women regarding how to speak to their husbands and take every thought captive to obey Christ. She tells them about her own experience of praying that the Lord brings to mind the right and timely words in the right tone. She tells of how regular and specific prayer for this has recalibrated her mind to resist the temptation to be rash or foolish in speech. Instead she has become an example of sweet speech with the teaching of kindness on her tongue (Proverbs 31).

But asking the Lord to bring the right response to mind in the moment of temptation must also be combined with meditation. Notice that the devotion of the blessed man in Psalm 1 manifests itself in *habitual meditation*. 'On his law he meditates day and night' (v. 2). If your biblical antennae are up you'll be already thinking of God's instruction to Moses' successor Joshua, 'This Book of the Law shall not depart from your mouth, but you shall *meditate on it day and night*, so that you may be careful to do according to all that is written in it' (Josh. 1:8). God says, 'Meditate on my Word.' This word for meditate means 'to chew over' or to 'mutter': muttering Scripture was a common practice.

Be careful where you do this, but I recommend it! This is true meditation. Muttering the Scriptures and as you do setting them in your mind, the verse, the order, the meaning, the application. This is how you hide the word in your heart. What does the psalmist say in Psalm 119:11? 'I have stored up your word in my heart, that I might not sin against you.'

How will a young man keep his way pure? 'By guarding it according to your [God's] word' (Ps. 119:9). Don't meditate on your iPhone or pornography or PlayStation. Meditate on God's Word. Let it sink into your mind. Don't let it depart from your mouth. Mutter God's Word – but don't grumble *against* God's Word. Make this godly muttering your regular habit. 'But that's not cool', some might say. No! What's not cool is a generation of young men addicted to pornography and who don't fear the Lord. It's the same for young women. It's the same for all of us. What do you meditate on most? What is on your lips most? What are you muttering about?

Prayerful meditation on the Bible helps us with lust. Instead of a woman dwelling on all the things her husband is not and focusing on all the things another man is, and wandering into an emotional affair, she takes every thought captive to Christ. She takes a psalm and prays through it and lets the Word of God shape her emotions. The result is that she moves from discontent with her husband and dwelling on lustful fantasies to praise and thankfulness for her husband and love for God.

No doubt, sexual purity is particularly difficult for single Christians who may be tempted to lust and masturbation. But prayerfully focusing on all the treasures they already have in Christ, meditating on what sex is for and in what sphere it is good (marriage) is the power for purity.

(v) Avoid temptation

Avoiding temptation is a key wisdom strategy in the fight against lust. Firstly, be watchful. You have an enemy and he is a roaring lion, seeking to devour your faith (1 Pet. 5:8). You must also deal with the enemy of your own sinful lust which is crouching at the door.

It is folly to underestimate Satan and sin (as we saw in Chapter 3). But the Scriptures tell us to deal with them in different ways. When it comes to the devil, fight him face to face. Peter says, 'Resist him, firm in your faith' (1 Pet. 5:9). But Paul says, when it comes to youthful lusts, 'flee.' Get out of there and put distance between yourself and it (2 Tim. 2:22). Don't flirt with this sin. Give sin no quarter. Otherwise it will quickly seduce and overcome you.

In that 2 Timothy passage Paul says that a person should flee lust but also *pursue righteousness*. There is much wisdom in a man or woman knowing their purpose as a Christian and planning to pursue it. Unthinking Christians who are without a plan often coast, and Christians who coast often crash. Planning your week helps avoid temptation moments. Remember how King David found himself lusting after Bathsheba. He wasn't doing what a King should be doing. He should have been away with his troops in battle. Instead he was wandering on a rooftop and lusting after a woman who wasn't his wife.

Secondly, know what places and people to avoid – like being alone with a member of the opposite sex. This was Billy Graham's practice. The 'Graham rule' has been criticized in some quarters as being over cautious and unnecessary. It is not surprising that this is so, for in our modern world, the boundaries of work and home—coworkers and spouses—have in some cases gotten very blurry indeed. Some fall into the trap of caring more for the advancement of their career than for the integrity of their marriage. For the Christian, no such tradeoff is advisable. While there may be times when one-on-one meetings have to happen at work, our goal is always to put our spouse first, and to protect the marriage—and our sexual purity, whether married or single—God has given us. While not an explicit biblical teaching, Graham's practice has much to commend it.[5] Extended time spent alone with a member of the opposite sex is a recipe for disaster and a breeding ground for lust.

In terms of what to avoid we can get further wisdom from Psalm 1:1.

> *Blessed is the man*
>> *who walks not in the counsel of the wicked,*
> *nor stands in the way of sinners,*
>> *nor sits in the seat of scoffers.*

The blessed man 'walks not in the counsel of the wicked.' He avoids being influenced by the rhetoric, aims and principles of the wicked world – those who are not Christian. Such is the pull of the wicked, and the deceitful schemes of Satan, and the remaining sin in our own hearts, that we

---

5   Graham adopted this practice after his ministry expanded, and he and his team observed prominent evangelists—who traveled widely as Graham did—destroying their marriages through adultery far from home. See Grant Wacker, *America's Pastor: Billy Graham and the Shaping of a Nation* (Cambridge, Massachusetts: Belknap/Harvard, 2014), pp. 10-11, 141.

are in danger of beginning to walk in the counsel of the wicked if we are not vigilant. If you listen to enough worldly talk about sex you begin to get desensitized to its wickedness, and you begin to walk with the idea. But the blessed man avoids the counsel of the wicked.

Notice also, the blessed man does not 'stand in the way of sinners.' He avoids the way of sinful living. If you expose yourself to sexual imagery, what you could not stand the thought of you now stand the thought of and begin to travel on the way of sinners. And it's a broad way – an easy road, with lots of fellow travelers, but it's a way that leads to destruction. So the blessed man is in the world but not of the world and he avoids the way of sinners.

The blessed man also, does not 'sit in the seat of scoffers.' These scoffers are the people who are so indifferent to God that they hate divine things. They are mockers of creation, marriage, morality and all that is decent and honorable in the eyes of God. They call good evil and evil good. They say sex outside marriage is okay, pornography is okay, transgender is okay, and homosexuality is okay. They are often clever, articulate, powerful and popular and make fun of Christians and Christianity. The blessed man avoids that seat.

Look carefully and you'll see the development of spiritual failure here. You walk: at first you listen to and toy with sinful ideas. It's maybe not visible to others at this point. But soon you stand in a habit of sin. It has become a lifestyle. Now it's visible. Finally you sit. You're stuck, rooted, addicted. This is the way it is with lust; like spiritual creeping paralysis, moving from walking to standing to sitting: from motion to motionless. Nevertheless, the psalmist's wisdom on avoidance builds resistance to the crippling effects of lust.

One further word. On the idea of avoidance, know what other barriers to put in place – like Covenant Eyes on your computer. Know your own weakness. There are perhaps certain situations that are not themselves sinful but for you seem to be the circumstances which foster lustful feelings. It might be something as simple as staying up late alone when others have gone to bed. Or it could be loafing around the house in boredom rather than being actively engaged in righteous pursuits. It could be carelessly scrolling through Instagram accounts or YouTube videos – you're never more than a few inches from serious temptation on social media and the Internet. In fact, I often tell young men that laziness is the manure in which sexual immorality grows. (That doesn't fail to get their attention.)

(vi) Practice turning at first impulse

One particular skill my dad taught me as a child was the art of turning with a soccer ball. I was never going to be tall, so he would take me into our back-yard in Southeast London and teach me how to quickly switch directions with the ball at my feet. 'The big guys won't be able to catch you!' he said. For hours I would practice turning to the left and right, until I didn't even think about it in a match. It came naturally. My dad was right: the art of turning served me well. Many of the goals I scored in the years to come were a result of that lesson.

This is the technique and practice we need to build into the battle against lust: turn from sin at the first impulse. Don't justify the feeling because it was uninvited and just a reflex. As covered in Chapter 2, it is still sinful and needs to be confessed and turned from. It may feel awkward. But sincere and consistent practice will train the mind to sever sin at the root. The more you train yourself in this practice the more you begin to do it naturally, instinctively. You will develop healthy sexual reflexes.

A young man whom I counselled for his lust problem several years ago thanked me for instilling this practice into his life. He said, 'I remember at one point we discussed whether the uninvited lust desire was sinful. That really confronted me because I had justified my sinful thoughts and actions because of my desire. My identity was wrapped up in my sexual desires: "This is who I am". And I began to excuse the impulse. To turn from lust you must first see the impulse as sinful.' This young man gained great victory by practicing the art of turning at first impulse.

I believe you will as well.

(vii) *Practice gratitude in all circumstances*

The flip side of this counseling was not only to practise turning at the first impulse of lust but also to practise gratitude in all circumstances. Ephesians 5: 3-4 is particularly instructive here: 'But sexual immorality and all impurity or covetousness must not even be named among you, as is proper among saints. Let there be no filthiness nor foolish talk nor crude joking, which are out of place, but instead let there be thanksgiving.'

In verse 3 Paul warns against sexual immorality and the unrestrained sexual behavior that impurity implies, and he connects this with covetousness. Outward actions begin with inward, greedy cravings of the heart (note the Bible's consistent revelation of the origin of sin – the heart). In verse 4 he goes on to mention sexual sins of speech, i.e. filthiness, foolish talk and crude joking.

Now if we look carefully at the text we will see that Paul offers an antidote to this catalogue of sexual sin. It's called gratitude. 'Instead let there be thanksgiving.' In other words he wants gratitude to replace these things. They can't exist together. Christians who have experienced God's grace and generosity towards them in Jesus Christ must be marked increasingly by gratitude. So gratitude undercuts self-centered sexual lust. The more we practice being thankful in all circumstances the less we will experience lustful impulses in the heart. They will be crowded out by gratitude.

(viii) Look at Jesus

You cannot lust, and love Jesus, at the same time. You cannot look at porn and look at Jesus simultaneously. So the ultimate power to kill lust lies in the person of Christ Himself holding sway in our hearts. We saw the gospel in terms of our union with Christ in Chapter 3. The Apostle John tells us that the reason that we will be made perfectly like Christ, resurrection body and all, is that we shall see him face to face (1 John 3: 2). The union becomes face-to-face communion at the consummation of all things.

When we wander into sin we always wander away from a person. That person is firstly, Christ. So we must work to see His power and beauty, wisdom, righteousness and grace, so that He becomes more compelling to us than sin or anything else. We do not want to cut out lust without filling the void with Christ. To put it in the 'spiritual surgeon' language of our previous chapter: we cannot cut out the disease from our sinful heart without applying the healing balm of the grace of Jesus. If we leave a lust free wound open, it will soon become infected with another sinful infection. But seal it with Christ instead. Let there be no room for sin in your heart because Christ dwells there (Eph. 3:17).

You see, we don't want to stoically avoid pornography but secretly be desiring to watch it. What we want is not to desire to watch it at all because it tastes bad to us now. We want it to appear to us 'like a gold ring in a pig's snout' (Prov. 11:22), because that is the way Jesus sees it ... and we are looking into His eyes.

So how do we increasingly cultivate the reality of the person of Christ in our lives?

Here is one way. Read and meditate on the Gospels—that is Matthew, Mark, Luke and John—regularly. In these eyewitness accounts we have the most concentrated portraits of the person of Christ in His life on earth. In the Gospels, Jesus cannot be reduced to a theological concept. He is the flesh and blood God-man who died for me. I see Him in His human interactions and in divine communion with His Father in heaven. I hear Him on the cross cry 'Father forgive them' and realize He was speaking about me. I see Him in His resurrection body promise to return as He ascends to heaven and I know He is coming back for me. I hear Him warn me about the reality of hell and the narrow way of sanctification. And I hear Him encourage me with rock solid promise filled with tender patience 'I am with you always, to the end of the age' (Matt. 28:20).

It's the beauty of Christ in all He is that makes Him the most important person in your life, and that is what encourages us in the fight against lust: because union with Christ is less about union and more about Christ. It's about knowing that His love holds onto you and nothing can separate you from it. And when you fill your vision with Christ there's no room for lust. It pales into insignificance – it shrivels up and dies.

As the famous hymn puts it:

> Turn your eyes upon Jesus
> Look full in His wonderful face
> And the things of earth will grow strangely dim
> In the light of His glory and grace.[6]

This is the right instinct. He's the point of our lives. He's the focus of our days. He's the antidote to our sins.

We end where we began: when you boil it all down, a book about lust is really a book about Jesus.

---

6   'The Heavenly Vision', Helen H. Lemmel, 1922.

FREQUENTLY ASKED QUESTIONS

What Does The Bible Teach About Lust?

In this section of the book, we address questions people frequently raise surrounding the issue of lust. Our aim here is not to give lengthy and exhaustive answers to these good queries, but is instead to build off of the content of this book and give short, readable, practical guidance on these subjects. We cite Scripture as our authority and guide, but in some answers below, we give biblically-shaped wisdom where there are gray areas.

1. In this Internet age when does a parent teach their children about pornography?

This is a wisdom call. There is no specific text that tells you what age you should do this if at all. But we are told that parents are to bring children up in the discipline and instruction of the Lord (Eph. 6:1-4 cf. Deut. 6:7). This means teaching them the biblical worldview of creation and sexuality in age appropriate language in order not to confuse or alarm them and not to awaken love before its time (Song 8:4). But parents are to protect their children from harm in the world in which we live today. This is very different to forty years ago. The average age of a child being exposed to pornography is around eleven now and probably getting younger. Sex is so accessible and normalized in movies and music that we need to be particularly vigilant.

Three things we suggest. First, instruction in the Scriptures: if the Word of God dwells in them richly it will help keep their way pure. Second, restriction of devices: don't let children have free and unrestrained access to the Internet on phones and computers. Install parental blocks and have computers in open spaces. Third, vigilance over friends: encourage the kind of friendships that will promote purity in your children rather than destroy it.

2. How do we avoid lust when we are engaged?

Firstly, make the engagement as short as possible. Avoid the now-common cultural practice of marrying years after one's engagement.[1]

---

1   Too often we hear of Christian couples who must wait a year or two before their wedding. We encourage fathers and mothers of children who want to marry, and give evidence of readiness for marriage in the adult years, to not delay the marriage of their children for long.

Once you are engaged the emotional desire ramps up, so there is no need to postpone the wedding and put unnecessary moral strain on the relationship. Secondly, treat her 'like a sister in all purity' (1 Tim. 5:2). The Bible has only one category as the context for sexual thinking, touching and acting – marriage. She is not your wife until you are married and he is not your husband until you are married. Until then they are just a brother or sister in Christ. This means no passionate kissing or touching. (Some Christians will see room for some display of affection given that the couple is to be married, but such should be lined out with great care and regular accountability.) These are the parameters we suggest, which guard the mind and body and honor God. Avoid situations that might tempt this – prolonged time alone together, for instance. Thirdly, turn the question on its head and ask, 'How can we best glorify God in our engagement?' You will then view biblical prohibitions as biblical positives.

3. Why is masturbation sinful? Is abstinence from this asking an impossible standard from single men and women?

Some Christians have adopted a position that masturbation is a morally neutral act; others have adopted a view that it is acceptable if there are no sexually immoral thoughts in the process. But it is quite clear that masturbation does not serve procreation or consummation. It is not other-centered love, as sex within marriage should be (1 Cor. 7 her body is for him and his is for her), and it is extremely unlikely that it can be achieved without sexually immoral thoughts. So it falls short of God's divine purposes for sex. Solo sex is a form of self-love and it is also habit forming. Most men and women have engaged in it and it is not just an issue for singles. But it is an immoral use of sex.[2]

We don't believe that it is an impossible standard for single men and women, but it won't be easy. Nevertheless God never calls us to do something for which He won't supply the power. We remember God's words to the Apostle Paul; 'My grace is sufficient for you, for my power is made perfect in weakness.' And so Paul can say, 'Therefore I will boast all the more gladly of my weaknesses, so that the power of Christ may rest upon me' (2 Cor. 12:9).

---

2   We commend the searching and biblically-rigorous article by Jason DeRouchie of Midwestern Seminary on this topic: 'If Your Right Hand Causes You to Sin: Ten Biblical Reflections on Masturbation,' December 3, 2016, accessible at https://www.desiringgod.org/articles/if-your-right-hand-causes-you-to-sin. Last accessed January 2020.

4. Is a lust problem, such as pornography addiction, grounds for divorce? Is it abandonment and/or adultery?

Generally, we don't think so. Jesus speaks in Matthew of a man who lusts and commits adultery in his heart. But it is not exactly the same as adultery in the same way anger at a brother is not the same as murder. Though his addiction means he has to some extent abandoned his role as a husband it is not exactly the same as leaving his wife. Even in these cases of adultery and abandonment for which the church has allowed divorce (and Jesus permits it), we strongly recommend an attitude that seeks reconciliation.

With that said, we recognize the grievous sin involved here and the hugely damaging effects it has on a marriage. So we might see a situation where the lies and betrayal of trust have so decimated the relationship that a period of separation might be permissible and beneficial. The addict should certainly be in counseling. They should receive marital counseling too.

If this does not prove workable, and if the sin simply does not stop, then the use of porneia in Matthew 19:3-6 does—as some theologians and pastors interpret it—allow for the possibility of divorce, for porneia is not limited to an adulterous act, but is a broad term for sexual sin.

5. You say that the lust impulse is sinful and requires repentance – isn't that demoralizing for the believer who doesn't want to lust and is fighting hard?

We empathize with all who seek purity in an impure world. This is no easy journey to glory, and we are carrying our cross on the narrow way. Yet we do well to remember that for every saint, our yoke is easy and our burden is light (Matt. 11:30). The world, the flesh, and the devil pull at us all in many ways, but Christ is not a cruel master, and our union with Him (see Chapter 3) means we have all the strength and encouragement we need to make it safely home.

This means that those who struggle with lust of any kind are in the same category as any other redeemed person. We all have what we need to gain victory, the Word of Christ (Col. 3). There is no Christian who does not need to attack sinful impulse at their root level not just their fruit level. We are all battling sin together, fighting temptations (internal and external) of many kinds. Yet we must never make the mistake of thinking that some believers are in a different category than others, or have a different identity than the mainstream evangelical. We all need Christ desperately, and we must all fight sin vigilantly. There is no other kind of Christian than this.

6. Can you expand on what repentance from lust looks like?

It doesn't necessarily mean a zero experience of ongoing lust. We wish it did! But we must be honest about our failings. While we do not have zero experience with temptation, we do have a zero tolerance approach to both the impulse and the action – we must flee from this sin (2 Tim. 2:22) and tear it out (Matt. 5: 29). It also means a constant vigilance on the issue – being watchful (1 Cor. 16:13, cf. 1 Peter 5:8). But you will also bear fruit in keeping with repentance, so it will be visible, not just in an absence of viewing pornography for instance but also in a diminishing of desire for viewing pornography as time goes on and as the Spirit works in your heart. Sanctification is both positional—we are made holy at conversion—and progressive, developing over the course of a lifetime.

7. I used to watch pornography regularly and by God's grace I don't now. But I still have lustful dreams sometimes. Am I sinning and is there hope that the dreams will stop?

Even when we have recent experience of sin and have victory in that area there is often consequence from that original event of sin or pattern of sin. In the case of pornography it might be images in the subconscious that once seen cannot be unseen. These might emerge in dreams occasionally. We would differentiate from the unchosen or un-invited impulse when we are awake in that when you are awake you are conscious. But we do think it is a sinful picture within the dream. We also believe that the power of the gospel is such that if we pursue purity and pray for God to relieve us of this burden he can do so.

So, in sum, we would not counsel undue con-demnation over unasked-for dreams (provided one is fighting for purity in one's waking hours). We would, however, encourage repentance whenever we find ourselves drifting into ungodly fantasies, whether conscious or asleep. You could pray some-thing like this: 'Lord, you know I did not want that dream, but it happened. Please forgive me, and please continue to renew my mind so that I dwell on what is pure, excellent, beautiful, and pleasing to you, whether waking or sleeping' (Phil. 4:8).

8. What should you do if a church member confesses watching pornography to you?

Well to begin with it is a good thing that they confessed. After which it requires wisdom to know the next steps. Presuming they are of the same sex you might be the one to provide ongoing counsel to them. If you don't feel able then referring them to an elder would be appropriate but the work of the elders is to equip the saints for the work of ministry (Eph. 4:11-12). The eight steps provided in this book give a good framework for how any ongoing counsel might look. If the person is in ministry leadership they ought to step down for a while and in that respect the elders should be informed. Restoration to ministry in such instances should not be hasty, but should be handled carefully, with all due patience and caution, and without certain expectation of resuming leadership.

Along these lines, pastors who follow their lusts into addiction and adultery should step away from ministry for a solid block of time (at the very least). Godly exegetes debate whether restoration of a pastor or elder who commits adultery—as one example—is preferable or even possible. For our purposes we would simply say that gross sexual sin (whether as a pattern or a stand-alone act) should be treated with tremendous care. Pastors who break their marriage vows (whether through pornographic addiction or a consummated affair) should operate under the general expectation that they have forfeited their ministry and need to find other work. We do not want to say that it is impossible for such men to return to ministry, but we do want to say that a return is unlikely at best.

9. Should elders ask the question about pornography at members' interviews?

We do (Gavin). It is something we have begun to practice in more recent years because this issue is so prevalent and many people are living with un-confessed sin here. A person regularly using porn does not qualify for church membership because it is a contradiction of their profession of faith. That person would need to show consistency in repentance and mastery over pornography before being given entrance to church membership. If a person confessed to this sin whilst already in church membership, then the answer would be according to Question 8. If a person confessed to this sin prior to an application for church membership, we would recommend an accountability and counseling with an elder or someone of spiritual maturity with the aim of restoration and fitness for membership.

10. How should a married couple keep each other pure?

Paul recommends regular intimacy except for a time of prayer (or menstruation) (1 Cor. 7). It affirms the marriage covenant on each occasion of sexual union and it is an expression of joy in your spouse. Thus you are training the body and mind to work sexually towards your spouse alone. Spiritual disciplines, like word, prayer, and church are also a basic protection for standing firm in the faith. It is likely best to be accountable to a friend or fellow church member, and to be honest but discrete about temptation with one's spouse. There is variance here among believers, but we want to do what we can to encourage our spouse while never glossing over hard truths with them.

11. How do you rebuild trust after your spouse has confessed to being addicted to porn?

Be willing and be wise. If the gospel has gripped our hearts we will be willing to forgive our spouse. We must. But this doesn't mean that things will automatically become good between you. Wisdom means the couple will address the issues at heart and take the necessary counsel and time. The offending spouse needs to be very honest about his or her motives behind their sin. The fact that there was pornography addiction points to deeper issues in the marriage relationship. This by no means lays the blame on the non-offending spouse. But in a wider sense he or she must be willing to work on other issues. For instance the offending spouse might say that the sullen attitude and non-communication of their spouse was influential in them seeking a sense of acceptance through porn. The silence and sullenness did not make them sin, but it is something that is not right and needs addressing at root level for the rebuilding of the marriage and deeper trust. To achieve the rebuilding of trust both parties will need to clothe willingness and wisdom with humility.

12. If I want to find a church that preaches and teaches the doctrine this book unfolds, how can I find one?

We hope and pray this happens as a result of this little book. God loves the local church, and calls us to join one in membership (see Matthew 18; 1 Corinthians 5; Hebrews 10:25). We would encourage you to find a church that clearly and happily affirms the following: the Chicago Statement on Biblical Inerrancy, the Danvers Statement on Biblical Manhood and Womanhood, and the Nashville Statement on Biblical Sexuality.

13. If we tell the truth about the sin of lust, won't non-Christians tune us out, causing us to lose our witness?

There is no tension between telling the truth and loving fellow sinners. It is loving, in fact, to tell the truth. Our proclamation of God's teaching, then, does not get in the way of Christian witness. Christian proclamation *is* Christian witness. We need to supplement our speech with the fruits of the Spirit, to be sure. We cannot think that we should only speak up and do no more. We are called to be 'light,' after all, to shimmer with life and love and the beauty of holiness (Matt. 5:17-20). But do not be mistaken: the natural man does not receive the things of God (1 Cor. 2:14). People may well disagree with, dislike, and even despise us for telling the truth about homosexuality. They could even go so far as to persecute us, as happened with Christ, as happened with His apostles, as has happened to countless Christians over the centuries.

Come what may, we must not lose sight of the fact that we are called to speak the truth in love. There is no new mission for Christians today; there is no new way for the church to proclaim God's Word. Pastors must lead out in this great calling; if our pulpits are mighty in the Scriptures, our people will be mighty in the Scriptures.[3] It is true that our own context may have its own sinful predilections, but we must not overdo

---

3   To better understand how every pastor is called to be a theologian, see Kevin J. Vanhoozer and Owen Strachan, *The Pastor as Public Theologian: Reclaiming a Lost Vision* (Grand Rapids: Baker Academic, 2015).

'contextual' witness. While always taking stock of where we are, we must remember that every place and every people has a truly desperate need for God, His gospel, and His Word. This is what the church gathered is in business to provide; this is what the church scattered strives to declare.

In the end, we will not be measured by results in themselves. We will be measured in divine terms by faithfulness to the Word of God, not any earthly metric of popularity, fame, or success.

14. You've given practical counsel in Chapter 4 of this book, but as a counselor or discipler in the church I want a fuller 'method' by which to walk people through gospel transformation and the everyday fight for faith. Any suggestions?

This book is a partnership; the method below is one we have worked out together based on sound biblical doctrine, and that Gavin in particular has identified and applied in his pastoral work with numerous men and women. We call it the 'Delineation of Desire' approach.

1. **Discern** if the person is a Christian or not. This makes a huge difference. If they are Christian they need discipleship and counselling. If they are not they need evangelism and conversion. The first thing anyone needs is Christ. If they are saved they

then, as a new creation, have the spiritual ability to go on being transformed by the renewal of their mind (Rom. 12:1-2).

2. **Draw** the person out. Gather information about their background and current life situation. This shows that when you speak the truth you love them as a person made in the image of God and don't regard them simply as a project (Eph. 4: 25). It is also valuable in seeing what outside influences there have been upon their sin, and if there are certain trigger situations where their sin manifests itself regularly.

3. **Detail** the significance of the gospel and what union with Christ means. If not a Christian, call them to faith in Christ. If they are a Christian, re-mind them that God could never love them less or more than he does in that moment, that their sins are forgiven and there is no legal guilt for them anymore. And that they have both the freedom and the power to overcome sin and put it to death. But also remind them that they must do this.

4. **Delineate** the design. As we have discussed, take people to the framework of biblical sexuality. Apply their situation to the good and wise design of God, and show them how faith in Christ affirms divine creation for all who are a new creation in Christ.

5. **Detect** the flesh. This flows from point two. Knowing the person and their story helps detect

what might be underlying sins beneath the sin. (Sometimes sins cluster together, and sometimes they come on their own, even as all sin is idolatry.) In light of the previous point and a clear understanding of sin, identify what drives their specific sin patterns: is it desire to be worshiped, fear of man, envy, vengeance, power that underpins the sin they manifest?

6. **Destroy** the sin. Once the person has identified sins beneath sin they are in a position to kill sin at root. Realising their union with Christ they can name the sin(s) and turn from them. This repentance must happen at impulse level.

7. **Draw** near to Christ. Put on Christ – put on the new self (Col 3). The Bible is specific about putting on Christ and becoming that which we are in Christ. Help the person see in which particular areas they need to grow: gratitude (key with sexual sin), humility, patience, joy and so on. Show them how being in Christ produces this in them.

8. **Direct** them to regulate their Christian life with regular times in the Word and prayer, leading them to pray specifically that God would help them take all desires and thoughts captive to Christ (2 Cor. 10:5). Also encourage wise inclusion of others to whom they might be accountable in their fight for purity.

9. **Determine** to walk with them them in the fellowship of the church, knowing that sin is stubborn and change can take time. And above all pray. Spiritual change is supernatural change. True, the person must work – that is non-negotiable. But as Paul says it is God who works in a person providing the ultimate transformation (Phil. 2:12-13). Therefore, it is to God that we appeal and in His sovereign grace we rest.

ACKNOWLEDGEMENTS

We wish to thank Willie Mackenzie for his partnership in this book. The team at CFP was characteristically excellent in their work on the project; we thank them for all their labors, with a special word of gratitude to Rosanna Burton.

Erik Wolgemuth provided terrific literary representation in this endeavor.

We thank the leadership of Midwestern Baptist Theological Seminary (Kansas City, Missouri) and Calvary Grace Church (Calgary, Alberta) for their support, and for slotting us roles that allow us to serve the church through writing. Dr Jason Allen is an exemplary seminary President, and Clint Humfrey is an exemplary pastor-theologian.

Our wives, Bethany Strachan and Amanda Peacock, persevered in a jam-packed writing season and offered encouragement throughout the process. We each send love to our wife.

This book is dedicated to two pastors who either led us to Christ or showed us the way of Christ from an early age. We are grateful for these men and their influence in our lives.

Above all, we thank the living God, and pray that He may continually strengthen us and find us faithful on the last day.

About the Center for Biblical Sexuality

The Center for Biblical Sexuality (CBS) is a new initiative from Owen Strachan and Gavin Peacock. Primarily a website featuring resources on manhood, womanhood, biblical sexuality, the family, and more, the CBS offers biblical and theological clarity on the most pressing issues facing the global church in the areas of the body, personal identity, and sexuality. The mission statement of CBS: 'To strengthen the church and share Christ's love by answering pressing sexual questions with sound biblical doctrine.'

At the website, visitors will find long-form articles, multimedia content, links to helpful sites, and more. Please visit this new outlet at centerbiblicalsexuality.org.

Also available by Owen Strachan and Gavin Peacock...

What Does the Bible Teach About Homosexuality?

A Short Book on Biblical Sexuality

Owen Strachan & Gavin Peacock

God made sexuality. It is a gift and stewardship from God. But His purpose for our sexuality has been distorted by sin. Gavin Peacock and Owen Strachan encourage us to look at what God says about homosexuality, but also at the glorious truth of Christ's defeat of sin and redemption of our identities.

978-1-5271-0477-8

What Does the Bible Teach About Transgenderism?

A Short Book on Personal Identity

Owen Strachan & Gavin Peacock

Gender identity is a controversial and complex topic. Owen Strachan and Gavin Peacock dive into the subject with biblical clarity and the clear message of the gospel.

978-1-5271-0478-5

Christian Focus Publications

Our mission statement —

STAYING FAITHFUL

In dependence upon God we seek to impact the world through literature faithful to His infallible Word, the Bible. Our aim is to ensure that the Lord Jesus Christ is presented as the only hope to obtain forgiveness of sin, live a useful life and look forward to heaven with Him.

Our books are published in four imprints:

CHRISTIAN FOCUS

Popular works including biographies, commentaries, basic doctrine and Christian living.

CHRISTIAN HERITAGE

Books representing some of the best material from the rich heritage of the church.

MENTOR

Books written at a level suitable for Bible College and seminary students, pastors, and other serious readers. The imprint includes commentaries, doctrinal studies, examination of current issues and church history.

CF4•K

Children's books for quality Bible teaching and for all age groups: Sunday school curriculum, puzzle and activity books; personal and family devotional titles, biographies and inspirational stories — because you are never too young to know Jesus!

Christian Focus Publications Ltd,
Geanies House, Fearn, Ross-shire,
IV20 1TW, Scotland, United Kingdom.

www.christianfocus.com
blog.christianfocus.com